SCOTTISH MILITARY UNIFORMS

BY THE SAME AUTHOR

British Artillery on Land and Sea, 1790–1820

Scottish

Military Uniforms

ROBERT WILKINSON-LATHAM

DAVID & CHARLES · NEWTON ABBOT, LONDON, VANCOUVER

HIPPOCRENE BOOKS INC · NEW YORK

HIPPOCRENE
BOOKS, INC.

This edition first published in 1975 in Great Britain by
David & Charles (Holdings) Limited, Newton Abbot, Devon,
and in the United States of America in 1975 by Hippocrene Books Inc., New York
Published in Canada by Douglas, David & Charles Limited, 132 Philip Avenue, North Vancouver BC

ISBN 0 7153 6633 5 (Great Britain)
ISBN 0-88254-314-8 (United States)

Library of Congress Catalog Card Number: 74-18970

Set in Monotype Bembo
and printed in Great Britain
by Biddles Limited, Guildford

Designed by John Leath

Contents

Author's Note

Although this book is entitled *Scottish Military Uniforms,* it does not include details of the Scots Guards or the large numbers of yeomanry, volunteers, militia and fencibles of Scotland which existed throughout the eighteenth and nineteenth centuries before being incorporated as volunteer and militia battalions of the line regiments in 1881 and incorporated into the Territorial Force (later renamed Territorial Army) in 1908. For uniforms of the Scottish Volunteer Forces, the reader is directed to *Records of the Scottish Volunteer Forces 1859-1908* by Lt-General Sir James Moncrieff Grierson, KCB, CVO, CMG, which shows some 230 different uniforms in colour (this rare book has recently been reprinted).

FOR

Christine and Edward

Acknowledgements

The writing of this book would not have been possible without the help, kindness and advice of a number of people who gave freely of their time and knowledge. I would especially like to thank W. A. Thorburn, curator of the Scottish United Services Museum, Edinburgh, who besides supplying illustrations and information read the text and corrected me on a number of important points. I also owe a special thanks to Boris Mollo and his staff of the Reading Room at the National Army Museum, London, for supplying photographs, photostats and other information. Captain R. G. Hollies-Smith of the Parker Gallery, London, in his usual helpful way allowed me free access to the negative files of the Gallery and advised me on the choice of illustrations.

ILLUSTRATIONS

The line drawings are by Christine Wilkinson-Latham and Jack Cassin-Scott, and the recruiting poster (fig 4) by J. Sheridan.

The plates are reproduced by courtesy of the following

Army Museums Ogilby Trust, London: 36
British Museum, London: 1 and 11
HM The Queen: 2, 8 and 13
National Army Museum, London: 4, 17, 21, 24, 25, 33, 34, 35, 44 and 46
Parker Gallery, London: 3, 5, 6, 7, 9, 10, 15, 16, 18, 19, 20, 27, 29, 31, 37, 38, 40 and 41
Scottish United Services Museum, Edinburgh: 12, 14, 26, 30, 34, 39, 47 and 50
Wilkinson-Latham Collection: 22, 33, 48 and 49

The following illustrations are taken from *Navy and Army Illustrated* (various volumes)
    28, 42, 43 and 45

Chapter 1 Cavalry
1742-1914

1742-1811

This account of the uniform, dress and equipment of the only regular cavalry regiment of Scotland does not commence with its founding but at 1742. However, the following few paragraphs will serve as a brief history of the regiment up to that date.

In 1678, three independent troops of dragoons were raised in Scotland and employed in collecting the local taxes, prosecuting non-conformists and 'to search out meetings in the open air'. In 1681, three additional troops were raised and the six embodied into one regiment styled 'the Royal Regiment of Scots Dragoons'. Independent troops of horse (the term used to describe heavy cavalry at this period) were also embodied as one regiment. Other independent companies were formed into two regiments in 1691, the first being Cunningham's, which, through the influx of English officers and men in 1745, became the 7th Dragoons and lost all connection with Scotland. The second, Newbattle's, was disbanded in 1697. Other independent companies formed into regiments suffered the fate of disbandment: Carmichael's, raised in 1694, was disbanded in 1698; Hyndford's, raised in 1702, was disbanded in 1713; and Cadross's, raised in 1689, was disbanded the following year.

In 1707, as a result of the union of England and Scotland into one kingdom, the regiment was restyled

the 'Royal Regiment of North British Dragoons'.

As with other regiments at this early period after the Restoration the uniforms did not conform to any particular pattern or colour. In February 1683, General Dalzell found that he could not 'be provided in this kingdom [Scotland] with as much cloth of one colour as will be clothes to the regiment of dragoons' and he was given permission and a licence from the Privy Council of Scotland to import '2,536 ells of stone-grey cloth from England, for clothing the said regiment of dragoons'. However, by 1687 the regiment was wearing red coats.

By the time of the Marlborough campaign at the beginning of the eighteenth century, the regiment was wearing red single-breasted coats, with round blue cuffs decorated with button loops and buttons. The coat had no collar and was buttoned up, showing only the neck cloth. The head-dress at this period was the tricorn hat, with the edge bound in tape to stiffen it and to act against wear and tear. High boots were worn over breeches and stockings, with knee protectors reaching to just above the top of the boot.

A move towards standardisation had taken place in the dress of the army in 1727 when the King ordered that uniforms should become 'fixed', differing only in facing colours, and that the 'several colonels' should prepare patterns. By 1729, the type and amount of clothing and the frequency of issue had been regulated. Each dragoon was allowed a new hat, 'cloth coat well lined with serge', waistcoat, breeches, large buff leather gloves with stiff top and a pair of new boots every four years or 'at such times the Colonel shall find it necessary within the four years'. Other items such as housings and cloaks were given out every six years and saddlery as and when required.

During the early part of the century, grenadier troops had been added to some dragoon regiments in the same way that grenadier companies had been attached to line infantry. Naturally, in their role as mounted grenadiers, they wore the embroidered grenadier cap.

By 1742, when the Duke of Cumberland's *Representation of the Cloathing of His Majesty's Household and All the Forces upon the Establishment of Great Britain and Ireland* appeared, only the Royal North British Dragoons and the 1st and 2nd Troops of the Horse Grenadier Guards were wearing the embroidered mitre cap with stiffened front.

The 'Cloathing Book' shows clearly the dress of another rank of the regiment at 1742 (plate 1). The coat is red and cut full with narrow collar and long skirts. The lining is in blue, and this is shown on the inside of the skirts which are buttoned back. The cuffs, round with a cut-out on the outside, are also blue with, above, a slashed panel displaying four buttons. The coat is single-breasted with twelve buttons and small button loops laced in white. On each side below the waist were slashed panels with white tape in chevron shape with a button in the centre. White tape button loops also appeared at the back, each side of the centre vent. Although some of the above description of the coat cannot be seen in the plate, an actual coat in the Scottish United Services' Museum supplies us with the details of the 'hidden' parts. A plain red shoulder strap was fitted to the left shoulder and a white shoulder knot to the right. The buff shoulder belt, whitened with pipeclay – and a unique feature at this period – had a large brass buckle on the front and a red flask cord over it, which held the priming flask above the ammunition pouch. The breeches are depicted as blue, as is the waistcoat. The cloak is red, lined with blue, and was rolled with the lining outermost.

The grenadier cap is shown. It had a red front, piped in yellow, with embroidered designs on it. The back part is also red with a blue head-band. A blue flap and the front displayed a thistle motif and regimental motto. An actual cap in the Musée de l'Armée, Paris, gives us much more detail concerning the design of the embroidery. Officers' caps were embroidered in gold and silver wire, while those of the other ranks were in worsted. The red front

was piped in yellow for the rank and file but was edged in gold for officers, for whom the material at the front was in velvet. In the centre of the front was the red cross of St George surrounded by the Garter belt and the motto 'Honi soit qui mal y pense', the whole superimposed on two crosses, one Latin and the other that of St Andrew, the former in worsted and the latter in white metal. Between the arms of the cross there were rays, also in white metal. On each side of the central design was foliage of thistles and roses in gold and silver. The small blue cloth flap on the front was also edged in gold and embroidered with a thistle under a scroll inscribed 'Nemo me impune lacessit'. The rear of the cap was red, piped in gold, with the turned-up band in blue.

In 1751, a royal warrant was issued describing in some detail the head-dress and clothing of the regiment, and by studying this in conjunction with the series of paintings of the British Army executed by David Morier (1705–70), a fairly accurate picture can be obtained of the appearance and clothing of the Royal North British Dragoons in the middle of the eighteenth century. The following extracts from the royal warrant apply to the regiment.

> The Royal North British Dragoons, only, to wear caps instead of Hats, which Caps are to be of the same form as those of the Horse Grenadier Guards; the front Blue with the same badge as on the Second guidon of the Regiment; the flap red, with the White Horse and Motto over it, *Nec aspera terrent;* the back part to be red, and the turn up blue, with a Thistle embroidered, between the letters II.D. being the rank of the Regiment.

The badge referred to as borne on the second guidon was the thistle 'within the circle of St Andrew'. The Morier painting, which was probably executed before 1751, shows a cap that does not conform to either that of 1742 or the 1751 version. The colour of the front appears to be blue with a red back but blue turn-down band. The thistle has disappeared completely from the embroidery, the small red flap now displaying the familiar Hanoverian horse and motto. In the centre of the front are the two superimposed crosses and the Garter belt and motto, still with red cross of St George in the centre. The 1751 cap is shown in fig 1.

The dragoon coats were without lapels and double-breasted. The cuffs were in the regimental face colour and slit on the outside. The pockets were described as 'long' and the buttonholes were to be edged in yellow or white lace, with the buttons set in pairs or threes. The waistcoat

PLATE 1 *Trooper, Royal North British Dragoons, 1742 (from the* Representation of the Cloathing etc . . .*).*

FIGURE 1 *Officer's embroidered mitre cap, Royal North British Dragoons, 1751.*

and breeches were to be in the colour of the facings and a yellow or white worsted shoulder knot, worn on the right side, was to distinguish the dragoons.

Rank distinction for sergeants and corporals was by means of narrow silver or gold lace, sergeants having it on the lapels, turn-ups of the sleeves and the pockets, while they also had silver or gold shoulder knots. Corporals, on the other hand, had the lace on the turn-ups of the sleeves and the shoulder straps but this time the shoulder cords were in silk.

In the *General View of the Differences, and Distinctions of the Several Corps of Cavalry etc* . . . the various regimental distinctions for the 2nd, or Royal North British Dragoons, were as follows:

Colour of Buttonholes and how the Buttons are set on. – white, 2 and 2.
Colour of the Housing and Holster Caps. – blue.
Colour of the Lace on the Housing and Holster Caps. – royal lace.
Badge or Device on the Housing and Holster Caps. – Thistle within the circle of St. Andrew.

Most of the above details can clearly be seen in the Morier painting (plate 2), which also shows the red cloak

with blue lining, rolled inside out, and the broad white belt with buckles and white ammunition pouch – at this date without flask or flask cord. The officers had silver lace and embroidery on their appointments in place of the white for the men.

Although the warrant of 1751 makes no mention of hats, but of caps only, for the regiment, various sources, including an Orderly Book in possession of the regiment, and inspection returns make references to hats, which were presumably worn on numerous occasions to preserve the embroidered caps which were an expensive item of dress. On 22 January 1759, for example, the regimental Troop Orderly Book stated: 'A stiver to be stopt from each man for having his hatt cocked, which the Major hopes the men won't be against paying as it is for their own advantage.' Later in the same year an order stated that the farrier was to cock all the new hats and the old ones were to be kept and used as nosebags. When the full-dress grenadier cap was worn in bad weather, the men were always ordered to put the oilskin covers on them to protect the embroidery.

In 1764 the regiment was ordered to be remounted with long-tailed horses, in place of those as shown in the Morier painting (plate 2). The subject of grey horses and their first use by the regiment has been a source of speculation for many over the years but it is impossible to find *exactly* when the regiment was mounted on grey horses only. Richard Cannon, in his *The Historical Records of the Royal Regiment of Scots Dragoons: now The Second or Royal North British Dragoons, called the Scots Greys,* put forward the theory that the regiment took over the grey horses that belonged to the Dutch troops of life guards of William III when they returned to Holland in 1699 but the earliest mention seems to be in 1694, when the King reviewed the regiment in Hyde Park before it embarked for the Low Countries and it was noted that the regiment was mounted on 'grey and white horses'. The *London Gazette* of 1706, in an article about the battle of Ramillies, refers to the regiment as 'Lord John Haye's Dragoons (the Greys)'. The *Scots Courant* of September 1715 stated that 'The Royal Regiment of Scots Grey Horses . . . marched from hence on Monday for Stirling.' The *Weekly Packet* for the same month refers to them as the 'Grey Horse', while the October *Flying Post* calls them 'Grey Dragoons' and in November 'the Scots Grey's.

In 1764 epaulettes were ordered to be worn by dragoons and dragoons guards: one on the left shoulder in lace or embroidery for officers of the regiment, a pair in the facing colour edged in silver lace with silver fringe for sergeants,

PLATE 2 *Trooper, Royal North British Dragoons, 1751 (from the painting by David Morier).*

silk tape and fringed in silk for corporals and in white tape with white worsted fringe for privates. At the same time the waistcoats and breeches were ordered to be changed from blue to white and the buttonholes on the waistcoat were ordered to be plain and without lace button loops.

These changes were incorporated into a new clothing warrant which appeared in 1768. The warrant ordered a new pattern of grenadier cap for the regiment, along the lines of that ordered in the same warrant for the infantry. It was described as being of black bearskin with 'On the Front of the Cap, the Thistle within the Circle of St. Andrew; and the Motto, *Nemo me impune lacessit'*. Although the new caps were ordered in 1768 they were not issued until 1779, when the name of each man was ordered to be placed inside.

The warrant described the coats for dragoons as being without lapels, with a single row of buttons, but having taped buttonholes each side. The cuffs were as usual in the face colour, not slit but with buttons on the sleeve 'set on Length-ways'. For the first time the collar or 'Capes' were ordered to be in the face colour and made to turn down but also on occasion to button up. The button loops for the regiment were white and set on in pairs.

On 21 September 1767, the War Office issued an order that at the next supply of clothing for the rank and file, and when officers required new ones, all buttons were to bear the rank of the regiment; but unfortunately the exact design of the early buttons of the regiment is not known – presumably they were in tin or pewter and bore the rank of 'II.D'.

The 1768 warrant detailed that sergeants were to wear 'Pouches as the Men do' and also a sash around the waist in crimson silk with a stripe of the colour of the facing of the regiment. Farriers were to wear blue coats faced with the regimental colour but those regiments whose coats were faced blue were to have red facings. The farriers were also detailed to have a bearskin cap but with a plate on the 'forepart of Silver-plated Metal on a Black Ground', which displayed a horseshoe badge. They were also to have 'Churns and an Apron'.

The men of dragoon guards and dragoons were to have 'Black Linen Gaiters, with Black Buttons with a small stiff top' which were worn for dismounted duties. Saddlery consisting of saddles, girths, surcingle bits and so on was ordered to be uniform and the bridoons to be black and made in such a way 'that the Horses may be linked with them when the Regiments are dismounted'.

In March the following year, it was ordered that those officers and men whose hair was too short were to be 'plated or club'd in the Style of the Horse Grenadiers' and they were ordered to provide themselves with 'false Hair of the Colour of their own Twenty-two inches wherefrom it is tied behind'. The same order also tells us that the 'Weast-coats fronts that was got in place of sleves to be given out to the men and immediately fitted to the Backs of the old Weastcoats'.

An interesting order concerning the change of quarters was issued on 15 June 1779 which detailed 'the Men to march out of Quarters in their New Cap, but when they return [sheath] their swords, they are to put their Hats on, and wrap their Caps in a Handkershief to prevent them from being Dusted. The Men are to wear their old Cloaths until further Order.' The new-pattern grenadier caps previously referred to were issued in Salisbury in October 1779 when an order stated: 'The new Grenadeer Caps to be fitted for the men, for which the troops are to parade in their lines tomorrow at ten oclock.'

The regiment was quartered in Durham in 1782 and in September the following order was issued:

The Horse Mains and Tails are to be Clean Washed & their Mains Plaited . . . On Monday . . . Next the men will trim their Horses as Short and neat as possible. The New Grenadeer Caps must be in the best Order, when great care is to be taken not to hurt the Enameling on the fronts of the caps.

As in other cavalry regiments hats were worn but usually only on dismounted parades, while the rest of the cavalry wore them at all times. The hat was ordered to be worn with 'the first Loop to be Exactly in a Line with the Nose – and the Hat worn as low upon the Brow as Possible'. Every man was also 'answerable for his present Hat – which is not to be given away or Disposed of till further order'.

Inspection returns also give a great number of details concerning regimental dress. For instance that of 1765 states: 'Worcester, November 13th. Two standards in bad condition recd in 1752. Officers have blue cuffs embroidered with gold, blue waistcoats and breeches . . .' The mention of gold lace for the first time indicates that although the privates retained white, the officers had switched from silver to gold.

In 1788, dragoon and dragoon guards were ordered in future to wear their sword belts slung over the shoulder and over the coats, the width being reduced from $4^1/_2$ to 3in 'to render the Appearance . . . more uniform'.

Officers on duty were to wear the belt in the same manner but when off duty and without sashes were to wear the sword belt over the waistcoat. At the same time as the new method of wearing the sword belt came in, an oval belt plate was adopted which fastened the belt on the chest. The design of this early pattern is, however, unknown.

In 1755, a light troop was added to the regiment to fulfil much the same objective as light companies-of-line infantry regiments. The uniform was similar to that of the rest of the regiment, except that a lighter style of cap was worn with embroidered front but with low rounded skull behind. In 1763, the light troop was disbanded and eight men per troop equipped as light dragoons. In 1778, after the outbreak of the American War of Independence, the establishment of the regiment was augmented by some 250 men and, as the regimental Order Book tells us, six men of the 'Augmentation' were to be equipped as light dragoons and therefore recruits of 5ft 5^1/$_2$in were to be allowed. The men equipped as light dragoons were six sergeants, six corporals and eighty-four men. In April 1779, the idea was dropped and the various light detachments from 7th, 15th and 16th Dragoons, together with those from the 2nd, were incorporated into a regiment numbered the 21st Dragoons. The men of the light section wore similar dress but with a round hat with low skull, ornamented with a metal front bearing the royal cipher and the rank of the regiment.

In 1782, at the suggestion of Lord Adam Gordon following an inspection of the regiment, the horse furniture was changed from blue to red. Two years later an inspection report noted that officers were wearing two epaulettes.

The problem of keeping the grenadier cap firmly on the head while mounted and riding at anything faster than the trot must have been a difficult one, as there were no chin-straps or cap lines to prevent loss. On 26 April 1789 the Orderly Book states that the colonel 'will give Half a Guinea to any Serjeant, Corporal, or Dragoon; who shall contrive the best Method of fixing on the Grenadier Caps, and easiest for the Men, so as in all Situations to prevent them falling off'. By this date a white feather plume was worn on the left side, directly copying the infantry grenadiers, and presumably the Hanoverian horse badge, which had disappeared with the all-cloth mitre cap, was placed on the red cloth patch at the back of the cap.

In 1791, carbines and bayonets were issued to the heavy cavalry in place of the long-barrelled muskets they had previously carried and in 1793 the white ammunition pouches were replaced by black leather ones. In 1796, a major change was made in the uniform of the regiment: its sword belts and sword. The sword belt, which had a frog stitched to the left lower part for holding the sword in its metal-mounted leather scabbard, was replaced with a belt having two slings, one long and one short, from which to suspend the new disc-hilted heavy cavalry sword in an all-steel scabbard. The clothing warrant of 27 July of the same year ordered the coats of the heavy cavalry to be made shorter – so as to clear the saddle – and to be buttoned all the way down the front, retaining the lace loops. The collar, cuffs and turnbacks were in blue and the sleeves made 'to button underneath', so that the coat could be easily put on over the sleeved waistcoat. Shoulder-straps were also in blue, with red cloth wings laced with white attached to them. These wings were reinforced with iron or brass plates 'of sufficient strength to resist sword cuts'. Buckskin breeches had been issued to the men in 1788 and a regimental order of September of that year, concerning the distribution of seizure money the regiment was to receive for its help to the Customs in seizing smuggled copper, added that 'Any of the men who are not provided with Buckskin Breeches, are to be furnished with them Previous to the Seizure money being Paid'.

In December of the same year the question of the uniform colouring of the breeches caused the order to be issued that they were to be coloured with a ball made from 1lb whiting and 2^1/$_2$lbs of ochre.

Plate 3 shows an officer of the period in this new uniform and with the bearskin cap with plate, peak and feather. The portrait shows the coat in scarlet with blue open collar and round cuffs, the former ornamented with two bars of gold lace, and the latter with two also, one on the blue cuff and one above. The front of the single-breasted coat is ornamented with eight visible bars of gold lace set in pairs. The wide sash knotted on the right side was crimson net and the white buff leather waist belt with gilt metal plate, bearing what appears to be a thistle, is strapped over it. The breeches are white and worn with knee-length boots. A white cross-belt is worn over the left shoulder, suspending a pouch behind, and each shoulder is protected with 'wing' epaulettes with either scales or interlocking rings.

In October 1802, an inspection report noted that the men of the regiment were wearing white stable jackets 'paid for by the men, price 11/–'. In watering order the men also wore 'Russia duck trousers'. Amongst the clothing and equipment issued to recruits there was a 'Powder Bag, Powder and Puff' intended for dressing the

PLATE 3 *Lt-Colonel Sir Thomas Hankin as a cornet, Royal North British Dragoons, c 1800.*

hair but in 1808 they were dispensed with when an order was issued that the men's hair, which had been plaited, turned up and powdered as grenadiers, should be cut short.

1811–1855

In 1811 there was a radical change in the uniforms not only of the regiment but the entire heavy cavalry also. The heavily laced red coat introduced in 1796 was abolished and one with shorter tails, no buttons and little lace substituted. The new coat had, for the 2nd, a blue collar and blue cuffs which were pointed in shape. A broad band of lace – yellow worsted for other ranks – was sewn to the front of the collar, down the front of the coat and around the skirts as well as outlining the pointed cuffs. There were no buttons down the front, the garment being fastened with a number of hooks and eyes. Leather breeches had been replaced by ones of plush and the bearskin cap had by this time been fitted with chin scales, the plate being changed from enamel to brass. The shoulder 'wings' had been replaced by epaulettes but with plain shoulder straps in red for the men.

The Royal North British Dragoons would have been dressed in the new uniform jacket earlier than other regiments at home as they were not involved in the drawn-out discussions on the various patterns of helmet which should be adopted. However, they did not receive their new clothing until October 1812, the Inspection Report dated May 1813 tells us, and they changed the lace on the other-ranks' jackets from white to yellow. This change-over was noted in the Inspection Report dated May 1812.

During the summer of 1812, web breeches were sanctioned and grey cloth overalls introduced which had, in the case of the Royal North British Dragoons, a blue stripe down the outside seam of each leg. Plate 4 by Hamilton Smith and aquatinted by Stadler (published in 1813) shows two troopers of the regiment wearing the 1811 coat. The larger figure in the foreground is wearing the white breeches and boots and gloves with stiff short tops as well as carrying the sword, carbine and plain black leather sabretache, suspended by two slings from the sword belt. The figure in the background is wearing the grey cloth overalls and the round valise and cross-belt with pouch and carbine swivel, which can be clearly seen. A prominent feature of the bearskin cap from the rear is the red cloth patch with white horse of Hanover. The red valise had been introduced in 1812 to replace saddle bags and bore the initials on each end 'R.N.B.D.'.

The officer's uniform was similar and plate 5 shows an officer of just post-Waterloo. The cut of the coat is similar as is the lace on the collar, cuffs and front. A crimson sash is worn about the waist, with the sword belt over it, and a white cross belt holds a pouch in the middle of the back. The overalls are laced down the outside seam of each leg and are reinforced on the inside of each leg with leather, clearly visible in the painting. The bearskin cap is similar to that of the other ranks, except that the lines were in gold cord and the plate gilt. The main difference between the cap in plate 4 and the one in plate 5

PLATE 4   *Trooper, Royal North British Dragoons in full dress and campaign dress, 1814 (from the* Costume of the British Army, *drawn by C. Hamilton Smith – Wrapper no 9 published December 1813).*

PLATE 5 *Officer, Royal North British Dragoons, c 1816.*

is the scroll above the plate. This bore the word 'Water-loo' and was accorded to all ranks. The red valise and red cloak can be seen on the horse, which has a docked tail.

In about 1819, the uniforms of the regiment changed once more. After Waterloo, the battle honour had been granted to the regiment and ordered to be worn on the cap and to figure on the guidons. Besides the honour, however, the regiment was also ordered to place an eagle on their guidons. This badge, which was later to figure prominently on regimental appointments was awarded because of the courage and daring of Sergeant Ewart who, charging with the 'Union Brigade', captured the 'Eagle' (the French term for colour because of the

Imperial eagle on the top of the staff) of the 45th Infantry after a fierce hand-to-hand fight with the officer carrying it.

The uniforms of 1819 were fully described in *Dress Regulations* of 1822, issued for the first time in that year. The dragoons and dragoon guards were grouped together as their uniforms and equipment were similar, differing only, as will be seen, in small things such as the placing and number of bars of lace. In common with the rest of the army, the closed Prussian collar was adopted, laced all round, with 'a laced loop and small button at either end'. A corporal wearing the new uniform is shown in plate 6.

PLATE 6 *Corporal, Royal North British Dragoons, c 1818, wearing the new uniform introduced post-Waterloo. There should be only eight bars of lace on the chest.*

The coatee described in *Dress Regulations* 1822 was in scarlet with blue collar, cuffs and turnbacks. It was single-breasted with eight lace loops on the chest, a lace loop on the 'dragoon' cuff and three above it on the sleeve. The skirts at the back were rounded and ornamented with four lace loops and buttons with the turnbacks 'held' by a regimental-pattern ornament in embroidery. The loops on the sleeve, cuff and turnbacks were to be 'herring-bone form', ie like a chevron.

An aiguillette was worn on the right shoulder with 'gilt engraved tags' in gold twisted cord with a gold strap on the left shoulder. Field officers bore their rank badges on the aiguillette. In full dress, white breeches, stockings and a cocked hat were worn but in dress, blue-grey trousers replaced the breeches and the bearskin cap replaced the cocked hat.

Plate 7 shows an officer dressed according to the 1822 regulations. The coat, with its laced front of eight equally spaced bars and the high laced collar, can be clearly seen. The blue round 'dragoon' cuff with three bars of lace and buttons are shown, as is the girdle of gold and crimson lace 'full three inches and three-quarters wide', with the sword belt of gold lace worn over it.

The sword, in its steel scabbard, is suspended by two slings from the gold-lace belt with its gilt buckle with royal monogram, while the sabretache is suspended by three gold-lace straps from the same belt. The sabretache was described in the 1822 *Dress Regulations* as:

> ... blue morocco; pocket twelve inches and a half deep, ten and a half wide at bottom, eight and a half at top; face fifteen inches deep, thirteen wide at bottom, nine at top, covered with blue velvet and edged with two and a quarter inch lace, shewing a light of blue velvet on the outer edges; a gold embroidered G.R. surmounted by a crown relieved in silver, and encircled with oak-leaves.

The sabretache in plate 7 has the addition of battle-honour scrolls, bearing the words 'Peninsula' and 'Waterloo'.

The pouch belt, worn over the left shoulder, was also in gold regimental-pattern lace with gilt buckle, slide and tip suspending a blue velvet-covered pouch of similar design as on the face of the sabretache in the centre of the back. The overalls were described in the regulations as being blue-grey with a stripe of cloth 'about one and a half inches wide, colour of facing' down the outside seam, but this was soon changed for gold or silver lace. NCOs and men had been ordered in 1822 to discontinue

PLATE 7 *Officer, Royal North British Dragoons, c 1820, wearing the new-pattern uniform later described in* Dress Regulations *(1822).*

the use of white or yellow worsted stripes on overalls and to adopt stripes in the regimental face colour but in 1827, for some reason (W. Y. Carman gives in *British Military Uniforms* the reason that they were prone to fading), a return was made to yellow or white worsted stripes.

In full dress, officers were ordered to wear a sword with gilt pommel and boat-shell guard but in undress a steel basket-hilted sword was worn. In undress, the sword belt was in white leather and the sabretache in black patent, as was the pouch.

The greatcoat, which was described as 'blue; with braided loops and slashed sleeves', was ordered by a circular memorandum of 11 November 1822 to be optional wear on ordinary occasions provided 'they are never worn at Quarters without the sword & sash; the cocked hat in the staff and the caps for regimental officers'. It was also stated that regimental officers were never to wear the greatcoat at cloak parades or duty 'when the men are ordered to wear coat or cloak'.

Officers' cloaks, like those of the men, were scarlet lined with white shalloon and the collar was in the regimental face colour.

Regimental staff officers wore 'neither aiguillette nor shoulder strap' and a cocked hat. They also differed in not wearing the sash, or girdle.

The uniforms of the other ranks were similar in style but replaced gold lace with yellow lace. The overalls were blue-grey with a stripe down the outer seam of each leg. The girdle was in yellow and blue worsted with a white sword-belt worn over the top. Other ranks also wore brass shoulder scales and wore a white carbine cross-belt and black leather ammunition pouch (plate 6).

In about 1827, the lacing on the front of the coats was removed. In 1830, when William IV ascended the throne, he immediately abolished silver lace and buttons for the regular army and ordered that in future all lace would be gold. Overalls were changed from grey to dark blue and other ranks' stripes were now in yellow worsted. In 1827, a new cap had been authorised for the regiment and this one was a simplified version of the earlier pattern. It is shown in plate 8, three of the series of paintings by A. J. Dubois Drahonet (1791–1834). The series of three paintings executed c 1832 shows the new uniforms and head-dress of the regiment at the beginning of the reign of William IV. The collar of the coat was now entirely in the facing colour, whereas the earlier pattern had only the front parts in blue and was heavily decorated with lace and a grenade badge for officers. The *Dress Regulations* of 1831 directed that the coat should have nine buttons of regimental pattern down the front. They were gilt for officers and bore the eagle on a tablet inscribed 'Waterloo' within a scalloped rim, although this use was unofficial until 1838. The skirts and cuffs were decorated with three bars of gold lace. Richly embroidered and fringed epaulettes were worn on the shoulders by officers and these were ordered to be 'boxed', that is to say they had the bullion fringe sewn down on to a former to prevent them from moving. The overalls were blue with a broad stripe of regimental-pattern lace down the outside seam of the leg. Plate 8 shows an officer of 1832 conforming to the 1831 regulations. The waistbelt holding the sword and richly embroidered sabretache was in regimental-pattern lace on morocco leather with a gilt square belt plate. The cross-belt in the same pattern of lace bore an embroidered pouch in the centre of the back. In the two companion plates (plate 8) by Dubois Drahonet, a trooper and sergeant are depicted. Both the other ranks and the officers are wearing a similarly styled cap in bearskin, with just the smallest part of the metal plate visible under the long fur and a large white plume fitted into a grenade plume-holder on the left side and curving right over the crown of the bearskin cap. At the right, just beneath the end of the plume, are the flounders of the cap lines.

PLATE 8   *Officer, sergeant and private, Royal North British Dragoons, 1832 (from paintings by Dubois Dronhet).*

The trooper is shown wearing the new pattern of coat with nine buttons with yellow worsted lace on the collar and three bars on the cuffs and skirts. The shoulders are decorated with brass shoulder scales. The waist-belt is wide and in white buff leather with a brass plate displaying the thistle design, while the cross-belt holds a large black leather ammunition pouch in the centre of the back and also a carbine swivel on the right hip. The trooper is wearing the white trousers worn on dismounted occasions.

The sergeant is wearing the same pattern of coat but with lace on the collar and his chevrons of rank backed with cloth in the regimental facing colour. He is wearing the right gauntlet only, so the bars of lace on the left cuff can be clearly seen. He wears the same pattern of waist-belt and cross-belt as the private and is wearing the blue overalls with yellow stripe.

In 1834, the plate on the front of the bearskin cap was abolished and in 1837 the button at the bottom of the skirt was ordered to be dispensed with. In 1843, white trousers were discontinued and the feather in the bearskin cap done away with. This last order was, however, rescinded and in 1845 permission was given for the feather to be resumed, provided that the expense was not charged to the men. In 1846, a further edition of *Dress Regulations* was published, the first of Queen Victoria's long reign.

It is worth quoting from these regulations as they describe the uniform that was, with minor modifications, worn by the regiment during the Crimean War, the first major war to shatter the long peace after Waterloo. Once again, dragoon guards and 'heavy dragoons' (this was to differentiate them from light dragoons) were grouped together. The coat was described as:

Coat – scarlet; collar, cuffs, and turnbacks of regimental facings, which in Dragoons Guards are to be of velvet, in Heavy Dragoons of cloth; – single-breasted, with nine uniform buttons in front; two loops on each end of the collar; turnbacks laced; embroidered skirt ornaments.

The 'Heavy Dragoons' had three loops of lace on the sleeve, 'The entire loop . . . not to exceed one inch and three quarters in breadth'. Epaulettes were in gold bullion and 'boxed' with the strap and crescent embroidered in gold on cloth for 'Heavy Dragoons'. Within the crescent each regiment bore its badge in silver embroidery. The regulations mention that 'The Second or Royal North British Dragoons, have permission to wear a bearskin cap

with a white hackle feather, nine inches long according to regimental pattern.' Trousers were dark blue with a gold stripe but for levee dress and in the evenings blue trousers with a scarlet cloth stripe were worn. The sword belt was in gold lace, two and a half inches wide, with a frosted gilt plate with burnished rim, bearing the crowned royal cipher 'V.R.' in silver, encircled with oak leaves. The sabretache was covered in cloth of the facing colour and edged with lace and had the royal cipher embroidered in the centre of the cloth with crown above, encircled with oak leaves; the pouch was ornamented in a similar manner and carried on a $2\frac{1}{2}$in wide gold-laced belt with gilt buckle, slide and tip.

In undress, the sword belt and pouch belt were white leather and the sabretache and pouch in black patent leather. The stable jacket was described as being in scarlet cloth and single-breasted, with small studs down the front, the jacket fastening with hooks and eyes. It was ornamented with gold gimp on the collar and cuff and laced all round the bottom, the lace forming 'bull's-eye' ornaments on each hip. Twisted gold cords were fitted to each shoulder.

The stable jacket worn by the men was in red cloth and similarly cut but with plain collar and cuffs in the face colour and buttons down the front. With the stable jacket was worn the forage cap which was in blue cloth with a figure of Russia braid on the top and an embroidered patent-leather peak. In the Royal North British Dragoons the band around the cap was yellow zigzag 'vandyke' band on a red background until the mid 1840s when white 'vandyke' on dark blue was adopted. Other ranks' forage caps were in blue cloth, without a peak or figure on the top and with the unique regimental-pattern band.

The dress shabrack was in blue cloth with square corners and, for dragoon regiments, edged with a single row of lace 'the same pattern as for the trousers' and embroidered with 'regimental device'. The other shabrack was black sheepskin with scarlet edging.

The uniform and horse furniture as regulated in 1846 is well shown in the painting (plate 9), which was executed in 1852. Notice how the sword belt is worn *under* the coat and that, around the waist, a sash in 'crimson and gold with pendent tassels' is worn over the coat, with the tassels falling to the right-hand side.

The regiment landed in the Crimea in September 1854 to join the allied army as the first heavy-cavalry regiment in the theatre of war. The uniform worn on 'active service' was exactly the same as previously described,

PLATE 9 *Officer, Royal North British Dragoons, 1852.*

except that the other ranks carried a haversack and water canteen slung over the body. By this time, the red cloth valise bore 'II D' on the ends rather than 'R.N.B.D.'.

Booted overalls were soon adopted in place of the plain cloth ones, as they gave added protection and enjoyed a considerably longer life under campaign conditions. A portrait of Captain Toosey Williams, one of the two officers who died during campaign, reproduced in Almack's *History of the Second Dragoons,* shows him in booted overalls. These are bound with leather around the bottom of each leg up to mid-calf length and inside the legs and up to the waist at the front and back.

The regiment remained in the Crimea until 1856, when they returned to England after suffering hardships and privations during the severe winter of 1854–5. The lessons learned at the expense of the soldier concerning the inadequacy of the uniform and equipment had already been noted and in 1855 a vast upheaval in dress, amongst other aspects of the army, occurred. Such a major

change-over little affected the troops in the Crimea until 1856, as the entire army had to be reuniformed in the new style, which was noticeably influenced by the French, our allies in the Crimea.

1855–1914

As for the other arms of the service the new changes introduced a tunic in place of the coatee. *Dress Regulations* of 1857 described the new tunic as scarlet, single-breasted with the collar, cuffs and piping down the leading edge in blue for the regiment. There was a low 2in-deep collar, rounded at the front, on which was worn the ranking of the officer. The cuffs were round, with a single loop of lace and button in the centre, and the skirts were ornamented with three loops of lace each side. Epaulettes were replaced by gold cords. The tunic collar and cuffs were edged with 'a quarter-inch the same material as the facings'.

23

The other ranks' tunic was the same design but with brass buttons with the regimental device which was an eagle on a tablet inscribed 'Waterloo' above the initials 'R.N.B.D.', all within a scalloped edge. This pattern had been introduced about 1835. Also, on the other ranks' tunics, gold lace was replaced by yellow worsted.

Trousers – as they were termed in *Dress Regulations* – were dark blue with a stripe of gold lace of regimental pattern down the outside seam for full dress but with a cloth stripe in yellow for undress and 'strapped with black patent leather or sealskin, as for men'. Officers no longer wore embroidered sabretaches, these having been abolished in 1854 (other ranks had not used their leather sabretaches since 1831) and the embroidered pouches were now replaced with ones having a solid-silver flap with a gilt crowned 'V.R.'. In the Royal North British Dragoons, the gilt eagle was placed on the flap of the pouch but the exact date of adoption of this 'unofficial' pattern is uncertain. The black leather sabretache, previously used for undress wear, was now adopted for all occasions when this item was worn. The eagle badge was adopted unofficially for use in about 1835 but was officially approved in March 1838 and the motto 'Second to None' in July 1839.

The stable jackets for both officers and other ranks were single-breasted, the officers' in scarlet and the men's in red cloth. The collar and cuffs were in the regimental face colour. The forage cap was in blue cloth and, for the regiment, it had for officers a 'gold band with vandyked edges and thistle pattern' while those of the men had the vandyked band in white cloth. The cloak was now described as blue lined with white shalloon, 'same pattern as sealed for rank and file'.

The regiment still wore the bearskin cap, which now appeared very much like those of the foot guards, almost devoid of any visible ornamentation. The regulations noted, however, that the cap had a white hackle feather 'nine inches long, thistle (gilt) on the front of cap, according to sealed pattern'. The plume holder was in the form of a grenade with the royal arms on the ball and a metal white Horse of Hanover was worn at the back of the cap, although hardly visible amongst the fur.

Regimental staff officers wore the same uniform but with the cocked hat, the quartermaster with a white drooping feather-plume and the surgeon and veterinary surgeon, black feather-plumes. The surgeon and his assistant also wore a black morocco-leather cross belt and pouch 'for instruments' in place of the gold-lace pouch-belt and silver flap-pouch.

The above uniform, with booted overalls, was worn until the late 1860s when a slight alteration was made in the pattern of lacing on the tunic and the booted overalls gave way to breeches and knee boots for mounted order and overalls without strapping for dismounted dress.

In 1874, *Dress Regulations* describe the new ornamentation on the officers' tunics. The collar was ornamented with a thin row of lace, top and bottom, for field officers but only at the top for other officers. The cuffs were pointed, and edged with gold cord forming a knot at the apex – a triple knot for field officers, double for captains and single for lieutenants. There were two buttons at the waist behind and the skirts were ornamented with a 'Scarlet flap on each skirt behind, with 3 buttons, and edged with the same material and colour as the facings and the skirts lined with white'. The shoulder cords were twisted gold cord and worn on each shoulder, retained by a small regimental-pattern button. The cloth of the collar and cuff in the facing colour was to be velvet in the dragoon guards but cloth in the dragoons. General Order 94 of 1876 stated that the height of the collar must not exceed 2in. The same order also approved a patrol jacket in place of the frock coat for regiments that elected to wear it. The 2nd Dragoons retained the frock coat for undress. Overalls were still in blue as were the breeches, both having gold-lace stripes on the outside seam of each leg.

The other ranks' tunic was made of scarlet cloth from 1870 onwards and was similar in cut and design to that worn by the officers, the single Austrian knot and other braiding being in yellow worsted. The shoulder-straps were in blue cloth edged in yellow cord and held by a small button. The cavalry other ranks were not affected by the change-over from regimental to general-service-pattern buttons and continued to wear their own respective patterns. Other ranks wore a white buff sword-belt around the waist with two slings for suspending the sword. They also wore a white cross-belt, with brass buckle, slide and tip across the left shoulder, suspending a black leather ammunition pouch in the middle of the back. The breeches in blue cloth had a broad yellow stripe down the outside seam of each leg and were worn with black leather 'butcher' boots. In marching order a haversack and canteen were slung across the body by straps.

General Order 28 of 1877 stated that officers of cavalry were to continue to conform to the pattern of cloak approved for rank and file, which was mentioned in the 1874 regulations as being of blue cloth with scarlet collar and lined with white shalloon. The general order, however, altered the lining to scarlet shalloon, except for some regiments but not including the 2nd Dragoons, and the collar of the cape was to be in blue cloth. The previous year, the regiment had abandoned its title of Royal North British Dragoons and restyled itself Royal Scots Greys, a title that had been used previously for some years. The buttons were altered and now had 'R.S.G.' in place of the 'R.N.B.D.'.

The officers shabracks were in blue cloth and cut square and edged in gold lace with the 'Royal Cypher and Crown embroidered in gold' on the forepart and 'Crown over thistle, within a garter bearing the motto "Nemo me impune lacessit", a scroll with the words "Second to none" under the garter and 2 D below. The thistle in silver.' The valise, in red cloth, 27in long with the regimental number and initial embroidered in gold on each end was worn behind the saddle until 1880, when General Order 105 abolished it.

Regimental staff officers continued to differ in their dress and the cocked hat was still worn in place of the bearskin cap. The quartermaster was noted as having a white plume, the paymaster, no plume and the veterinary surgeon a red plume. The medical surgeons no longer figured amongst the regimental staff as they were withdrawn in 1873 and formed into the Medical Staff Corps with their own uniform. The veterinary surgeon is noted in the *Dress Regulations* of 1874 as wearing a white patent-leather belt and instrument case 'of departmental pattern', which was in black morocco leather.

The 1874 regulations describe the regimental pattern cap as 'Black bearskin, 10 inches high; with a gilt thistle in front; and a gilt grenade on the left side, as a plume socket, bearing the badge of St. Andrew, with the Royal Arms above, and the word "Waterloo" below. Plain gilt burnished chain lined with black leather.' The plume, white and 9in high, curved over the crown of the cap.

The main alteration in the dress of the Scots Greys was in the ornamentation of the tunic and the removal of badges of rank from the collar to the shoulder strap. These are described in the *Dress Regulations* of 1883. The scarlet flap on the skirt was to be edged with gold cord and tracing and the shoulder-straps of flat gold cord bore the badges of rank. The regimental staff officers consisted only of the adjutant and riding master, who wore the uniform of their rank, and the quartermaster, who continued to wear the cocked hat with white drooping plume. Regimental paymasters had disappeared in 1878 with the formation of the Army Pay Department and

regimental veterinary surgeons were organised into the Army Veterinary Department in 1881.

From the 1840s the band of the 2nd Dragoons had been dressed as the troopers, with the exception of the plume in the bearskin cap. The plume was scarlet and extended up the left side and over the crown of the cap. The bandsmen wore no pouches and cross-belts but yellow aiguillettes on the right shoulder. The drum horse carrying the large kettle drums was white and the drum banners which encircled the kettle drums were in red cloth. This detail is shown in a print by M. A. Hayes, published in the Spooner series in 1843. Another noticeable difference between the troopers and the bandsmen was that the forage cap had a yellow vandyke band in place of the troopers' white and had a silver metal grenade on the front of the cap. The grenade badge was worn by the band on their pill-box forage caps and later on the peaked cap. It is still worn by the band on the peaked cap.

While the band is being discussed, the question of the white bearskin worn by the mounted kettle drummer ought to be raised. Legend had it that this white bearskin cap was presented by Czar Nicholas II of Russia in 1894, when he was appointed colonel-in-chief of the regiment by Queen Victoria. However, this myth is not upheld by regimental records or photographic evidence. W. A. Thorburn, now curator of the Scottish United Services' Museum, Edinburgh, first published the truth in the Edinburgh press and later in the *Bulletin* of the Military Historical Society (no 38, November 1959). According to contemporary correspondence quoted by W. A. Thorburn, nothing was presented by the Czar and the white bearskin cap was sanctioned as an experiment by Colonel Welby in 1893 or 1894. He disliked the cap and it was seldom worn until his retirement in 1896. The legend that the cap had been presented by the Czar was started by Drummer Booth, the kettle drummer who first wore it, although this was refuted by Welby. After 1896 it was worn on a few occasions and it was not until 1935 that Colonel Pigot Moodie decided that it should be used for all mounted ceremonials. The original cap was already in the Edinburgh Castle museum and a new one was made from goatskin. This cap perished during the 1939–45 war and the original was loaned for the Edinburgh Castle and White City tattoos in the 1950s. The present cap is another copy.

A photograph of 1894 shows Drummer Booth, in the white cap with scarlet plume, mounted on the drum horse wearing the new shabrack, an ornate affair with the

PLATE 10 *Sergeant-major, Royal North British Dragoons, 1874 (from a painting by E. Holt). In the background are other ranks of the regiment being led by the mounted drummer.*

crowned belt bearing the motto with a thistle within and the eagle beneath and flanked each side with the white Horse of Hanover and the initials 'II D' as born on the guidon.

In 1884 the regiment supplied a detachment consisting of two officers and forty-four NCOs and men as part of the camel corps for the Egyptian campaign. In this capacity the men wore grey tunics, Bedford-cord breeches and blue puttees. The white helmet was worn with puggaree and blue-lensed sun goggles. They also wore a bandolier and white waist-belt, as well as the usual water canteen and haversack.

Although the 1883 regulations stated that the shabrack was only to be used for regiments that had decided to retain it, the Greys continued to use the embroidered shabrack until it was finally abolished. The pattern worn during the 1890s was the same as that previously described. Other ranks wore a saddle-blanket.

The other changes authorised in the new *Dress Regulations* were the full-dress and undress pantaloons, which were to have a cloth stripe in place of gold, stated to be 'the same colour as those worn by the men' – yellow for the Greys. Trousers were also, for undress, to have a cloth stripe. Another new item that appeared under the 'Horse Furniture' heading was a head rope in place of the chain which was described as 'Rope, head, cotton'. This head rope is shown in plate 10, as is the rest of the saddlery.

At the turn of the century, full dress consisted of the bearskin cap, a scarlet tunic with blue collar and cuffs, both edged in yellow cord, the latter forming a knot at the apex. Blue breeches with a yellow stripe were worn with black 'butcher' boots on mounted duties and blue overalls with yellow stripes with 'Wellington boots' on dismounted duty.

In the last *Dress Regulations* of Queen Victoria's reign, issued in 1900, the plume is described as 10in high for the bearskin cap. It was noted that the 2nd Dragoons Guards wore steel spurs on all occasions. A new item was a girdle in gold lace, worn in place of the gold-lace waist-belt, which was now ordered to be in webbing and worn under the tunic.

A red 'Angola, tartan or serge' frock coat was introduced for undress wear with two breast pockets and 'Steel shoulder chains with badge of rank'. The regulation issued in 1904 added nothing new to the full dress but of course described the khaki service dress that now was a universal order of dress in the British Army. Undress for cavalry now consisted of the blue frock coat, worn with the girdle and peaked cap. In 1903, the white buff cross-belts and black leather pouches were abolished for wear in full dress for NCOs and other ranks.

All the complicated and picturesque orders, such as stable dress and drill order, had now disappeared from the cavalry and the small pill-box caps with vandyked band were now replaced by larger peaked caps. The stable jacket, a short single-breasted garment, was no longer in use and khaki was, as in the infantry, the universal service dress.

In 1914, the regiment abandoned its full-dress bearskins and scarlet tunics and donned khaki with breeches and puttees. On 4 August 1914 the Greys mobilised at York and landed in France on the 17th to form part of the 5th Cavalry Brigade. It was ordered that the grey horses of the regiment should be stained chestnut as camouflage and to prevent identification.

Chapter 2 Infantry
1739–1830

Kilted regiments   1739–1796

There had been Scottish regiments on the establishment of the British Army before 1739 but they were, for uniform and accoutrements, treated in the same way as the rest of the infantry of the line. In 1738, Lord President Forbes of Culloden formed the idea of using the proven fighting skills and instincts of the Highlander in the service of George II. The plan was put to Sir Robert Walpole, the Prime Minister, who whole-heartedly approved of the scheme. In 1739, the existing independent companies in the Highlands were augmented by a further four and embodied as an infantry regiment of the line, taking the number 43rd in order of precedence.

Independent companies had existed in the Highlands of Scotland since 1667 and had led an intermittent life until 1717, when those that still existed were disbanded. The role of these companies had been the maintaining of law and order amongst the clans and to 'keep the watch' for cattle thieves. The men so employed do not appear to have had any type of uniform but were dressed and accoutred in the usual Highland fashion. Presumably they also wore or carried some distinguishing badge or sign, such as a tipstaff, to show their authority but no trace of any details can be found.

Following the Jacobite rebellion of 1715, the peace was, if somewhat brutally, restored to the Highlands but

unrest still prevailed. In 1725, the 'Disarming Act' was passed which made it a penal offence for any Highlander to have, use or wear 'a broadsword or target [shield], winger or durk, side pistol, gun or other warlike weapon'.

In the same year, General George Wade ordered that six independent companies should be raised as part of the forces of Scotland. Three of these companies, under the command of Lord Lovat, Sir Duncan Campbell of Lochnell and Colonel Grant of Ballindalloch, were to have 114 men and the other three companies, under Colonel Alexander Campbell of Skipness, John Campbell of Carrick and George Munroe of Culcairn, were to have seventy in each. On 15 May 1725, General Wade issued the following order concerning the dress of these new companies:

> that officers commanding companies take care to provide a plaid clothing and bonnet in the Highland dress for non-commissioned officers and soldiers, belonging to their companies, the plaid of each company to be as near as they can of the same sort or colour.

In September, General Wade issued a further order urging the immediate implementation of his May order and adding,

> You are to send lists of the company every four months to the officer commanding the troops quartered in the

Highlands, viz, on the 1st January, 1st May and 1st September. The number of their badges to be put before each man's name and when you have cause to change any of your men or fill up vacancies you are to give the badge to the man who succeeds.

From the above two orders it can be assumed that the dress of the companies was not uniform enough to be recognised and that a plaque or badge of authority was issued to each man to prove his official status. The 1725 companies were organised on a more regular basis than those raised previously and it is possible that they were issued later with a red coat to distinguish them as government troops – certainly those raised during the 1745 rebellion wore red coats with yellow facings and linings akin to the 43rd Regiment.

As can be expected, recruiting for these companies was no problem. From the time of the 1725 Act, the only way a Highlander could bear arms was in the service of George II. Many men of good families joined the companies and it was not an uncommon sight to see one of them coming on to parade on horseback followed by two or three servants carrying his baggage, arms and equipment.

Highlanders loyal to the Hanoverian cause during the 1745 rebellion are recorded as wearing a red cross on a white ground on the left side of their bonnets, while the eighteen new companies raised in the same year adopted the uniform worn by the 43rd, but for a time appear to have worn their own clothes with the red cross on a white-ground badge on their bonnets, until uniforms were available.

The problem as to the design of tartan worn by the independent companies has baffled historians as references are few, nor are they detailed. The orders of General Wade in 1725 enjoin the 'plaid of each company to be as near as they can the same sort or colour'. This indicates that a uniform pattern was not issued, the men perhaps wearing their own kilts as most of the recruits for the pro-Hanoverian Highland companies came from the Campbell, Grant and Munro clans. However, in 1727, Lord Lovat wrote to the other company commanders announcing that a large quantity of tartan was available for those companies which required it and that the whole tartan for 'ye sex companies at 10 pence per yard', which indicates a uniform pattern of material.

It must be remembered, however, that tartan, now taken to mean the particular style of checked cloth worn by Highland regiments and clans in the kilt and plaid, was until recent times used by tailors to describe a particular weave of material. In *Dress Regulations for the Army*, 1900, the undress scarlet frock jacket was ordered to be made from 'Angola, tartan or serge according to climate'. It may well be that when Lord Lovat wrote about the quantities of tartan available, he meant to imply that a plain coarse cloth of a basic colour was available and not the decorative material now known as tartan. The 1745 companies were dressed in the same way as the 43rd and adopted their particular pattern of tartan.

Letters of service dated 25 October 1739 were sent to John, 20th Earl of Crawford, appointing him to command the regiment that the government had decided to form from the independent companies and in May 1740 the 43rd Regiment, consisting of a thousand men, was embodied into the line.

The first uniform adopted by the 43rd (in 1749 renumbered 42nd) is well shown in the plate from *A Representation of the Cloathing of His Majesty's Household, and of all the Forces upon the Establishment of Great Britain and Ireland,* 1742 (plate 11), and a number of other engravings of the same year. Such was the novelty of this new form of military dress that a number of foreign artists executed plates depicting the strange garb. The 1742 'Cloathing Book', although not fully corroborated by the other contemporary artists, shows a Highlander wearing a flat blue bonnet with a black cockade on the left side. Some artists of the period show the edging to the hat band in red and white – which some authors have taken as an elementary form of dicing, later to be a feature of Scottish military head-dress – but it is more likely that the red and white depicted by these artists was meant to show a form of draw-string for adjusting the size of the bonnet to the head. The 1742 'Cloathing Book' also shows a small red tuft on the top, a feature not shown by some contemporary artists.

The coat is depicted as red without lapels and lined in a yellowish buff colour and with buttonholes, untaped, in pairs. The cuffs were also in the lining colour and turned up with a flap above with three buttons. Beneath the coat, which was worn open, was a red waistcoat buttoned to the neck. These patterns were peculiar to the 43rd (and the independent companies) as was the belted plaid worn in place of trousers.

The belted plaid, or the breacan-an-fheilidh, was the combination of kilt and plaid in one. It required twelve ells of tartan, doubled, which was pleated in wide box pleats and fastened round the body with a belt at the waist, the lower part forming the kilt and the upper part being

PLATE 11   *Private, 43rd Highlanders (later renumbered 42nd), 1742 (from the* Representation of the Cloathing etc . . .).

FIGURE 2 *Plaid brooches:* (left to right) *92nd Foot, c 1820; 21st Foot (piper), c 1870; Highland Light Infantry (71st and 74th), 1881–1914; 42nd Foot, c 1820.*

fastened by a brooch (fig 2) to the shoulder and hanging down at the back forming the plaid. Colonel David Stewart in *Sketches of the Highlanders of Scotland,* published in 1822, described the belted plaid as being

twelve yards plaited round the middle of the body, the upper part being fixed on the left shoulder, ready to be thrown loose and wrapped round both shoulders and firelock in rainy weather. At night the plaid served the purpose of a blanket, and was sufficient covering for the Highlander.

The hose or stockings were made from white cloth, with red diagonal stripes edged in black, and seamed at the back, fitting the leg. They were held beneath the knee by a garter in scarlet about a yard long, which was wound around the leg and finished in a special knot or snaoim gatrain. Black brogue shoes with buckles were issued but on service in the Highlands the men, more often than not, wore light heelless shoes of untanned hide known as 'curan'.

The equipment and arms, as in the case of the earlier independent companies, were supplied by the government except for 'dirks, highland pistols and targets [shields]' which were either supplied by the colonel or the men themselves. The 1742 'Cloathing Book' shows the cross-belt over the right shoulder in black leather, fastened by a simple brass buckle on the chest, suspending the issue broadsword on the left hip. The waist-belt, also in black, was worn under the coat but over the waistcoat and held a large leather ammunition box on the right front with the flap decorated with a brass crown and G.R. cipher. The bayonet was carried in a frog on the left front and those men who chose to supply their own dirks and all-metal Highland pistols wore them on the waist belt and a small cross-belt respectively.

The sporran or purse was of plain leather with a brass

frame and fastening and was decorated with knotted thongs on the front face.

In undress, the feile-beag, or little kilt, was worn. This was made of six ells of single tartan which was pleated and sewn before being fastened around the waist with a small strap and buckle fitted to the kilt. Half a yard or ell was left unpleated at each end and these portions crossed over in front giving a flat appearance.

In 1743, a number of men were sent to London so that the King could see the uniform and appointments of the new Highland regiment. The men performed broadsword exercises and other arms' drill before the King and an assembled number of general officers so, according to the *Westminster Gazette,* 'as to give perfect satisfaction to His Majesty. Each got a gratuity of one guinea, which he promptly gave to the Porter at the Palace gate as they passed out.'

In March 1743, the regiment was ordered south to England amidst much suspicion by the men, who had, they thought, been enlisted only for service in the Highlands. The regiment was told that the King expressed a wish to see them and accordingly they marched, reaching London at the end of April. They found, however, that the King had already sailed for Hanover but they were reviewed in May by General Wade. A few days later, after rumours had been circulating that the regiment was to be sent to the American plantations, the men decided to march back to Scotland. They reached Northampton and there entrenched themselves but were persuaded to surrender without bloodshed. Being disarmed, they were marched to London where the mutineers were tried, three being condemned to be shot at the Tower.

Corporal Samuel McPherson, one of two brothers executed on Tower Hill, is the subject of one of a series of prints by Bowles of London. The corporal is the main figure with, in the background, the scene of his execution. He is wearing the uniform described in the 1742 'Cloath-

The Scottish Highlander. Un Montagnard d'Ecosse

This Plate is most Humbly Inscribed to the Right Honourable the Lord Semple by his Lordships most Obedient Humble Servant. Wm Meyer.

ing Book' but does not appear to have the buttonholes in pairs. He has, in addition, a shoulder knot in white worsted on the right shoulder as a mark of rank. The equipment, shown in the 1742 'Cloathing Book' as black, appears to be of untanned or buff leather as does the ammunition pouch. A private, in a companion print, wears a similar dress but without the worsted ranking knot, which is replaced by a plain shoulder strap of the same colour as the jacket to keep the shoulder belt in position.

In 1746, after the '45 rebellion, a further Act was passed (19 Geo II, c39, s17) which restricted not only the weapons but also the Highland dress itself. The Act was 'for the more effectual disarming the Highlands of Scotland; and for more effectual securing the Peace of the Said Highlands; and for restraining the Use of the Highland dress'. The Act went on to state that only 'such as shall be employed as Officers and soldiers' would be allowed to wear Highland dress (plate 12). The clans who had been pro-Hanoverian during the rebellion were allowed a little leeway in interpreting the Act but for the rest, the penalty for the first offence was six months' imprisonment, for the second offence, seven years' transportation – but shooting on sight seems to have been a frequent occurrence.

In 1747, the grenadier company of the 43rd and Loudoun's Highlanders, who were raised in 1745, were permitted to wear a bearskin cap in place of the embroidered cloth 'mitre' cap worn by infantry grenadiers. The pattern of cap is described in the 1751 clothing warrant and illustrated in the portrait of the grenadier of the 42nd, executed by Morier as one of his series showing the uniforms of the army (plate 13).

Loudoun's Highlanders, disbanded in 1748, wore a similar uniform to the 43rd (renumbered 42nd in 1749) but with white facings. The tartan also appeared to be similar but with the addition of a red overstripe.

The uniform shown by Morier in his painting of a grenadier of the 42nd has the pointed bearskin cap with a red flap at the front. It is not sure whether or not this was painted metal or embroidered material. It was decorated at each side with white worsted embroidery or paint and emblazoned in the centre with the crown over the G.R. cipher. The jacket was red and single-breasted with the leading edges decorated in regimental-pattern tape (which was white with two red stripes in it) and nine singly

spaced buttonholes and buttons also decorated with a loop of regimental tape. The turned-down buff-coloured collar was also edged with tape, as were the pocket flaps each side at the hip. The waistcoat was also single-breasted and edged down the front and around the skirt in tape. The belted plaid is shown with a red overstripe, which is thought to denote the grenadier company, although it was quite common for regimental pipers to have the addition of an overstripe in the regimental facing colour. The same pattern of equipment in black leather was worn as in the 1742 'Cloathing Book'. The short hose were white with diamond patterns in place of the red diagonal stripes depicted in the 1742 'Cloathing Book'.

The *Regulations for the Colours, Clothing, etc, of the Marching Regiments of Foot and for the Uniform Clothing of the Cavalry, their standards, Guidons, banners etc . . .* of 1751 said of the grenadier cap of the 42nd that 'The Grenadiers of the Highland Regiment are allowed to wear Bearskin-Fur Caps, with the *King's Cypher* and Crown over it, on a *Red* ground in the Turn-up, or Flap.'

In July 1758, by special warrant, the regiment was given the title Royal Highland Regiment of Foot in recognition of the King's satisfaction with the loyalty, courage and conduct of the regiment. Because of the change in title, the facings of the regiment were altered to blue, the colour worn by all royal regiments.

During their service in Canada between 1759 and 60, it appears that the belted plaid was only used in camp and that the small kilt was worn on most other occasions. The bearskin tufts, which had been ordered to be worn on the left side of the bonnets of the regiment – except for grenadiers – were ordered not to exceed 5in in length and to be inclined over from the left side to the crown. At this period, officers who were mounted wore white pantaloons and boots.

In 1757, two Highland regiments were raised and added to the line. The first was the 77th Regiment (Montgomery's Highlanders) under the command of Major the Hon Archibald Montgomery (later 11th Earl of Eglinton) and consisted of thirteen companies of 105 men each. They were embodied at Sterling and embarked for North America. The uniform was similar to that worn by the 42nd with, at first, red facings to the jacket, later changed to green. Officers wore silver lace and buttons on their coats. In 1763, when the war was over, the officers and men were given the choice of settling in America or returning home. The regiment was disbanded in 1763.

The second regiment raised in 1757 was the 78th Regiment (Fraser's Highlanders) under the command of

◁ PLATE 12 *Private, 42nd Highlanders, by G. Bickham, April 1747.*

PLATE 13   *Grenadiers, 40th, 41st (invalids) and 42nd Highlanders, 1751 (from the painting by David Morier). This plate shows the differences between Highland and line regiments' uniforms.*

the Hon Simon Fraser. The regiment, consisting of the same number of companies, sailed with the 77th to North America and was disbanded in 1763. The uniform was the same as for the 42nd but with light-buff facings.

A second battalion, wearing the same uniform, was raised for the 42nd in 1758. This was disbanded in 1763. The following year, 1759, a further three Highland regiments were raised, the 87th (Keith's) commanded by Major Murray Keith, the 88th (Campbell's) under the command of Major John Campbell and the 89th Highland Regiment (Duke of Gordon's Highlanders) under the command of Major Morris, the husband of the Duchess of Gordon.

The 87th and 88th were ordered to Germany where they fought with distinction under Prince Ferdinand. Little information exists concerning the uniforms of these two regiments but it is certain that they were similar to that of the 42nd, who had established the precedent for Highland military uniform. A portrait of Keith in military uniform shows green facings but, as the painting was executed some years after the regiment was disbanded, it cannot be taken as reliable evidence. However, a portrait (sold at Christies in 1961) of Captain James Gorrey, who served in the 87th from 1759 to 1763, shows the officer in the correct uniform and confirms that the facings were in fact green. The facings of the 88th are thought to have been buff or yellow. Both regiments were disbanded in 1763.

34

The 89th embarked for India in 1761 and remained there until ordered to Scotland and disbanded in 1765. The uniform had yellow facings and was the same as that of the 42nd.

In 1760, the 101st Regiment (Johnstone's Highlanders) was raised under the command of Sir James Johnstone of Westerhall. At the end of 1761, the regiment was used to reinforce the 87th and 88th and the officers ordered to recruit a further six companies. Once this was done, the regiment was numbered the 101st and placed under orders for Portugal but peace came before they sailed and the regiment was disbanded. The uniform was similar to that of the 42nd but with pale-yellowish-buff facings.

In 1761, the number of Highland regiments was increased by the raising of four more. The 100th Regiment, under Major Colin Campbell of Kilberrie, was ordered to Martinique, returned to Scotland in 1763 and disbanded. Details of the uniform are not known. The 105th was embodied at Perth in 1762 and given the title The Queen's Highlanders. The regiment was sent to Ireland but returned and disbanded in 1763.

Maclean's Highlanders, raised in 1761, furnished drafts for the other Highland regiments and was eventually disbanded in 1763. The 113th, also raised in 1761, was styled the Royal Highland Volunteers and presumably had blue facings on the Highland-pattern uniform. It was disbanded in 1763.

By the time the second clothing warrant was issued in 1768, there remained only one Highland regiment, the 42nd. The new warrant went into more detail concerning dress than the 1751 warrant but did not make any specific mention of the Highland dress of the 42nd. All grenadiers now adopted the bearskin cap (fig 3), although of different design from the earlier pattern worn by the 42nd.

Officers wore gold lace and, consequently, gilt buttons and gorgets while other ranks wore the regimental-pattern tape on their coats and pewter buttons. Sergeants of the 42nd had the unique distinction of wearing silver lace on their coats, in place of the plain white tape ordered for sergeants of the line regiments.

At the start of the war with the American Colonists, more Highland regiments were raised, a number of which were destined to remain on the establishment of the line infantry of the British army.

In 1775, a new regiment was raised and commanded by Colonel Simon Fraser of Lovat, who had previously raised the 78th Fraser Highlanders, disbanded after the Treaty of Paris in 1763. The new regiment was the 71st (Fraser's Highlanders). The uniform was typical of the

FIGURE 3 *Grenadier's mitre cap, 1768.*

military adaptation of Highland dress that had been established, with white facings to the coat and white tape with a red worm for the rank and file. Until the end of the American war, the 71st wore a red feather hackle in the bonnet, a distinction which was later reserved for the 42nd. The 71st was disbanded at Perth in 1783.

In 1775, a regiment was raised from Scottish emigrants in North America and discharged men of the 42nd, Fraser's and Montgomery's Highlanders, who had chosen to settle in North America in 1763. The regiment was uniformed and equipped 'in like manner with His Majesty's Royal Highland Regiment (Black Watch)' and was given the number 84th and titled Royal Highland Emigrants (84th) Regiment. Although the regiment should have been numbered immediately after the 71st, it was not until 1778 that it was, as promised, taken on to the establishment of the line infantry. The accoutrements of the regiment differed from the 42nd in the fur of the sporran. The 84th had racoon-skin purses, while those of the 42nd were made from badger. In 1783, the regiment was disbanded and those officers and men who chose to remain in Canada received a land grant.

Three more regiments were raised in 1777: Lord MacLeod's Highlanders (73rd Regiment), the Argyll Highlanders (74th Regiment) and the MacDonald Highlanders (76th Highland Regiment). The 73rd had buff facings to their Highland jacket and the officers had silver lace, buttons and gorgets. The tape adopted by the rank and file was white, with a red line at the edge. A second battalion was raised in the same year and embarked for Gibraltar where it took part in the siege while the 1st Battalion sailed for India. The 2nd Battalion returned to Stirling in 1783 and was disbanded. With the reduction after 1783, the 73rd was renumbered 71st, while in India, in 1786.

The 74th had yellow facings and the 76th had dark green, the officers wearing silver lace, buttons and gorgets. Both regiments were disbanded in 1783.

In 1778, a further three regiments were raised: the Atholl Highlanders (77th Highland Regiment), 78th Regiment and the Aberdeenshire Highlanders (81st Regiment). The 77th had green facings, officers wearing silver lace, buttons and gorgets, while the 78th wore dark-yellow facings and the 81st adopted white with silver lace, buttons and gorgets for the officers. The 77th and 81st were disbanded in 1783.

In 1780 a further battalion was added to the 42nd and despatched to India where it served until 1786. In that year, the government decided to send the officers and non-commissioned officers to England and to draft the men into other regiments. This was completely contrary to their terms of service and after formal representations by the commanding officer, the battalion was formed into a separate regiment and numbered 73rd (the 73rd was renumbered 71st). In most Highland regiments the terms of service forbade the drafting of men into other non-Highland regiments and this recruiting 'incentive' was usually printed on the recruiting posters (fig 4).

The control of the pattern of clothing and other matters for the army was maintained not only by the written clothing warrants but by a system of 'sealed patterns'. Once a certain item of clothing was approved by the King, it was 'sealed' with a wax seal of the arms of the Board of Ordnance and deposited at the office of the 'Clothing Board', where it could be inspected by the commanders of regiments and the clothing contractors who had received orders. The office of the Clothing Board – in Tooley Street, London – was destroyed with

its contents in 1750. The new offices holding the patterns were housed in the Tower of London from that date but these too were destroyed in 1841, when a fire gutted the Grand Storehouse.

The basic cut-away coat authorised by the 1768 clothing warrant was to remain, with slight variations, until the introduction of the short-tailed, fully buttoned jacket in 1796. At the beginning of the American war, all regiments, including Highlanders, were divided into battalion companies and flank companies, consisting of grenadiers and light. The battalion men and officers wore the cocked bonnet with a regimental-pattern button in the rosette on the left side on the diced band, while the grenadiers wore the authorised bearskin cap with metal plate. The light company wore what were described as 'Light Infantry Caps', which were round pot-type caps, reinforced with metal bands or chains and having a turned-up peak at the front.

An account sent to the paymaster of the 78th describes the caps as follows:

3 Grenadier Officers' caps, strong silver-plated fronts and grenades, rich silver lines and bullion tassels, complete at 73s. 6d., £11. os. 6d. and 3 Light Infantry Officer's caps, solid leather fronts and picks, black ribbon rosettes and silver-plated bugle-horns in front, at 14s. 3 large feathers for ditto at 3s.

The feathers worn in the side of the cap of both officers and men of the light company were green.

After 1780, the waist-belt was worn over the right shoulder, an order which did not seem to be popular with the Highlanders. In 1784, shoulder-straps which *should* have previously been red were ordered to be in the facing colour and for some regiments who had already changed, unofficially, prior to this date, the irregularity was authorised.

Information on the exact tartans of the various regiments is scarce but usually a variation of the government tartan or that worn by the 42nd was used, with the addition of one or more overstripes. The 73rd, for example, added a red and buff stripe, while other regiments contented themselves with adding only one overstripe, normally in the face colour of the regiment.

Because of wear and tear on active service, some modifications were always being made to the uniforms of the soldiers in making the best of what was available. An inspection report of the 42nd, while it was in Nova Scotia in 1784, stated that the regiment could not appear in full uniform because there were no suitable plaids as the

SEAFORTH'S HIGHLANDERS

To be forthwith raised for the DEFENCE of His Glorious Majesty KING GEORGE the Third, and the Preservation of our Happy Constitution in Church and State

All LADS of *TRUE HIGHLAND BLOOD* willing to shew their Loyalty and Spirit may repair to SEAFORTH, or the Major, ALEXANDER MACKENZIE *of Belmaduthy:* or the other Commanding Officers at Head Quarters at _____ where they will receive *HIGH BOUNTIES* and *SOLDIER-LIKE ENTERTAINMENT*

———————

The LADS of this Regiment will LIVE and DIE together;—as they cannot be DRAUGHTED into other Regiments, and must be reduced in a BODY in their OWN COUNTRY.

———————

Now for a stroke at the *Monsieurs*, my Boys!

KING George for ever!

———————

HUZZA!

FIGURE 4 *Recruiting poster of the Seaforth Highlanders, 1793.*

commanding officer had disposed of them during the war to buy more 'commodious dress for the American service'. The men wore their bonnets, red jackets, with 'Ticken' trousers and short black gaiters. There are also a number of instances when the plaid was made into trousers to suit local conditions or the men were issued with white trousers.

The 73rd, who embarked for India in 1779, wore the 'East India Uniform' consisting of white pantaloons and short black gaiters and, in place of the bonnet, the round hat or 'Mother Shipton'. Captain Innes Munro in his *Military Operation on the Coromandel Coast* stated:

> Our Regiment has found it impossible to wear Highland dress any longer in this country, we are therefore now clothed in white hats and trousers, apparel better suited to a hot climate; but I believe, notwithstanding this, that some of our soldiers would have braved the utmost rage of the musquitoes rather than quit their native dress.

This form of dress was also worn in the West Indies. The conical hat had a band of regimental tape or lace above the broad brim. In 1786, a War Office order of November directed that white hats should be worn in place of black ones for troops in India, while in 1798, black ones with false linings bound with black lace above the brim were ordered.

Most of the Highland regiments had been disbanded in 1783 but it was not long before the threats from the Continent, developing into the French Revolution and the Napoleonic Wars which followed, induced the government once more to seek regiments in the Highlands.

In 1787, the 74th Highland Regiment and the 75th Stirlingshire Regiment were raised. The former adopted white facings and the latter yellow. Both regiments were embarked for India to take part in the campaign against Tippoo Sahib and were issued with 'East India Uniform'. Both regiments served until 1806 when they returned to England. Although 'East India Uniform' was ordered for India it appears that the kilt often made an 'unofficial' appearance as the military authorities were forced to forbid the kilt as unsuitable for the climate of the country. Whether even this order was strictly adhered to or not is hard to say.

In 1793, after many unsuccessful attempts by Francis Humberstone MacKenzie of Seaforth, the government at last decided to accept his offer to raise a regiment. The 78th adopted buff facings to the Highland coat, the officers adorning theirs with gold lace and wearing gilt cross-belt plates, gorgets and buttons. The kilt was the government tartan with the addition of a red and white overstripe. The 79th Cameronian Volunteers (in 1804 retitled Cameron Highlanders) were also raised in 1793, adopting green facings with the officers' coats having gold-lace loops, set in pairs, while the men's were white, with red, green and red lines also set in pairs. The kilt deviated from the usual adaptation of the 42nd pattern and was a special design which, it was said, was taken from an old tartan and elaborated by Sir Allan Cameron of Erracht, the commanding officer. It became known as Erracht or 79th tartan.

In 1794, the 97th Strathspey Regiment, 98th Argyllshire Highlanders, 100th Regiment, 116th (Perthshire) Regiment and 132nd Highland Regiment were all raised. The 97th had green facings, the officers gold lace, gilt buttons, gorgets and epaulettes. The grenadier company wore the normal 1768-pattern cap with the regiment's number on the grenade at the rear. In 1795, the officers and men of the battalion companies were drafted into other regiments while the flank companies, grenadier and light were transferred to the 42nd on 28 November at Hilsea.

The dress of the 98th was described in an order dated 16 May 1794 as follows:

> Officers – Field dress, jackets or frocks (*scarlet* faced with *yellow*), hooked at the top through the shirt; cloth or cassimere vests; kilts or belted plaids; black velvet stocks with false collars; silver epaulettes; hair cut close and clubbed, well powdered at all parades, with rosettes on the clubs.
> Men – Full Highland dress; facings *yellow;* lace, *black* and *white;* yellow oval shoe-buckles; the kilt and plaid, *green* tartan with *black* stripes.

The 98th embarked at Spithead on 5 May 1795 for Cape Colony and prior to embarkation the men were issued with 'East India Uniform'. The feathers worn in the round hats are noted as being '*white* for grenadiers, *green* for the light infantry, and *black* for the battalion companies'.

The 100th also adopted yellow facings and the kilt was the same as for the 42nd but with a single yellow overstripe. As a result of the reduction in the number of regiments of the army in 1798, the 98th and 100th were renumbered 91st and 92nd. The other regiments raised the same year – 116th, 132nd and 133rd – were broken up before they were embodied and the men drafted into other regiments. Little information can be found about their dress but the 116th wore Highland uniform with white facings and silver-lace loops set in pairs on the coat, silver buttons, and epaulettes.

An accurate idea of the dress worn by Highland regiments before the drastic change from the open-fronted coat to the short-tailed single-breasted jacket in 1797 is shown in the paintings of c 1790 by Edward Dayes, draughtsman to the Duke of York. A pair of paintings in the series Dayes executed shows a sergeant and an officer of the 42nd. The sergeant (plate 14) wears a blue bonnet with diced border, amply adorned with black feathers fitted behind a cockade on the left side which appears to have a regimental-pattern button in the centre. The coat is lapelled in the face colour (yellow) and adorned with button loops which are bastion-ended, the lapels fastened at the neck with hook and eye and sloping away. The waistcoat is plain white, buttoned to the neck and the kilt is of government tartan. The sporran is badger-skin with the flap to the purse pocket in the form of a badger's head. The hose are red and white with a diamond pattern, tied below the knee with scarlet tape. Privates wore a plain leather or goatskin sporran, sergeants and officers retaining the badger's head pattern. The sergeant also carries a broadsword (abolished for the rank and file in 1776) and dirk, as well as a musket. The cross-belts were ordered to be changed from black to buff in 1789 in the 42nd (although other regiments continued with black leather belts until as late as 1798). The belt holding the sword was fastened on the chest with an oval regimental-pattern belt plate. The officers wear much the same style of uniform but with only one cross-belt and lace adornment to the coat, gorgets and sash.

The increasing size and number of the feathers adorning the bonnet had led to remarks concerning the expense entailed. In an inspection report of the 42nd for May 1790 it was stated:

The bonnets are entirely disfigured, they are so covered with lofty feathers that they appear like high Grenadiers' caps of black bearskin and are made by that means expensive to the men. Sergeants wore silver lace.

In some regiments, bearskin was issued in place of feathers while Colonel Mackenzie of Suddie, commanding the 2nd Battalion of the 78th, issued imitation feathers made of worsted, stating that they were superior to real feathers in that the bonnets could be made to look uniform in size and shape: 'Every one knows who is aquainted with the 42nd Regiment that their bonnets are the least

PLATE 14 *Sergeant, 42nd Highlanders, 1792 (from a watercolour by Edward Dayes). Notice the dirk and broadsword carried by the sergeant, the cocked bonnet with diced band and feathers, and the hose.*

uniformly dressed, and the worst part of their clothing and appointments.'

In 1791, field officers of all regiments were ordered to wear two epaulettes but this order had little effect on the Highland regiments who already wore two. At the same time, the bugle horn and grenade were ordered for the flank-company officers' epaulettes.

By 1794, it appears that kilts and plaid were pre-pleated by sewing, instead of the old method of pleating before putting on. This is probably because of the lack of men able to perform this complicated task since the abolition of Highland dress in 1746.

In 1796, a warrant introduced a short-tailed coat fastened to the waist for all infantry.

Kilted regiments   1796–1830

The new coat introduced was made so that it could 'either button over occasionally or to clasp with hooks and eyes'. The collar was now a stand collar with button and lace loop for the gorget (for officers only) and the epaulettes previously worn were retained. This was found to be too complicated for the rank and file and late in 1797 the coat was made single-breasted without lapels and with tape button-loops ornamenting the chest.

For the officers, the short-tailed coat was retained in Highland regiments. It could either fasten with hooks and eyes to show the facing colour of the lapels, could be fastened completely to reveal a double row of buttons, or could have the top few buttons left undone and the lapels turned back (plate 15).

Gorgets were, in the same year, ordered to be gilt for all regiments irrespective of their lace colour and they had by this date become smaller and less crescent-shaped. A Horse Guards' order of 28 October 1797 instructed Highland regiments in future 'to wear waistcoats of the same material and make as adopted by other regiments of infantry'. This garment was used as a fatigue jacket and survived in Highland regiments and the foot guards as a drill jacket until 1919.

By 1800, the number of line regiments had been reduced to ninety-two but in that year a further Highland regiment, the 93rd Sutherland Highlanders, was raised under the command of General Wemyss of Wemyss. The facings adopted were yellow with silver lace, buttons and cross-belt plate (officers) and white tape, bastion-ended with a green and red stripe. The 93rd tartan was the Black Watch or government pattern. Much later a tartan of lighter colour was used and called Sutherland because of the regiment's name.

The uniform of the soldier was divided into what was termed 'Cloathing' and 'Necessaries', paid for from deductions to the soldiers' pay, known as 'Off reckonings' which were handed to the colonel. Incorporated in the pay, 1s a

day in 1797, was an allowance of 6d for necessaries and messing was not to exceed 4s a week. *Regulations for the Cloathing of the Infantry* of 1801 ordered for 'Highland Corps' that 'Each Sergeant, Corporal, Drummer and Private Man should have annually a coat, a waistcoat or waistcoat front, a bonnet and four pairs of hose. Six yards of plaid once in two years, and a purse every seven years.' Greatcoats were also first issued in 1801 (priced at 10s 6d) and the following year chevrons were authorised – to distinguish the various ranks of NCO – and shoulder knots were discontinued. Sergeant-majors wore four in the same colour of lace as worn by the officers; sergeants wore three in white tape; and corporals wore two in regimental-pattern tape – all sewn to cloth of the regimental facing colour. In 1803, the clothing warrant ordered that the greatcoats of sergeants should have the collar and cuffs in the facing colour of the regiment and button of 'Sergeants' quality'.

In 1804, Henry Thorpe, then secretary to His Royal Highness, the commander-in-chief, wrote to Colonel Cameron of the 79th on the subject of the kilt, an item of Scottish uniform that had been the subject of much discussion and would always, during the next eighty odd years, be a bone of contention between the Scottish Highland regiments and the military authorities in London.

> Horse Guards 13th October 1804
> DEAR COLONEL, – I am directed to request that you will state for the information of the Adjutant-General, your private opinion as to the expediency of abolishing the kilt in Highland regiments and substituting in lieu thereof the tartan trews, which have been represented to the Commander-in-Chief, from respectable authority, as an article now become acceptable to your countrymen, easier to be provided, and better calculated to preserve the health, and promote the comfort of the men on service.

One can but wonder at the reasons which prompted this letter; perhaps it was the genuine feeling that trousers, even if made of tartan material, would be more suited to active service or perhaps the desire of the authorities to have the Highland Corps conform to the rest of the line. The real solution, in the light of what happened five years later, was that there were not enough recruits from the Highlands for the regiments on the establishment and that if 'Sassenachs' were to be recruited, as they were, it would be more popular if the kilt was not worn.

As would be expected, Colonel Cameron's reply must

PLATE 15 *Officer, 42nd Highlanders, 1808 (from a coloured engraving after J. Smith 1808). Note the elaborate sporran, the cross-belt plate and gorget. Notice the increase in the numbers of feathers on the bonnet when compared with plate 14 and the red feather worn on the left side.*

have scorched the paper it was written on. He went into lengthy discourse on the merits of the kilt for health and efficiency and the disadvantages, with regard to recruiting in the Highlands, if it was abolished. He ended:

... but I sincerely hope His Highness will never acquiesce in so painful and degrading an idea (come from whatever quarter it may be) as to strip us of our native garb (admitted hitherto our regimental uniform) and stuff us into a harlequin tartan pantaloon, which composed of the usual quality that continues, as at present worn, useful and becoming for twelve months, will not endure six weeks fair wear as a pantaloon, and when patched makes a horrible appearance – besides that the necessary quantity to serve decently throughout the year would become extremely expensive, but, above all, take away completely the appearance and conceit of a Highland soldier, in which case I would rather see him stuffed into breeches, and abolish the distinction at once. I have the honour to be etc.

(signed) *Alan Cameron*
Colonel 79th or Cameron Highlanders.

The Highland bonnet had now almost assumed the appearance it was to keep until the 1830s. The diced band, originally the draw-string for tightening, which had become purely decorative, was in red white and green, the 93rd, however, having only red and white and the 42nd, red, white and blue. The adjustment to the head was done by having two tapes at the back and a regimental order of the 92nd in 1796 instructed officers to see that the men's bonnets were complete with black ribbon at the 'V'-shaped slit at the back of the diced band so that they could be worn 'properly, and not down on their heads like a night-cap'.

The feather worn in the Hummel bonnet was the same as for the rest of the line infantry – red and white (with white uppermost) for battalion companies, white for grenadier companies (they ceased wearing fur caps about 1800) and green for light companies (caps were given up in about 1800). In the case of the 42nd, however, battalion companies wore an all-red hackle, a distinction awarded to the regiment in 1795 for its conduct at the battle of Geldermalsen on 1 January 1795. The light companies of the 42nd had a red top to the green hackle and grenadier companies had a red top to their white hackle. The rosette, fitted to the left side of the diced band, was adorned with either a badge – some honour badge, such as the sphinx on a tablet inscribed 'Egypt', awarded to the 42nd by George

III in commemoration of their victory over the French in Egypt in 1801 – or a regimental-pattern button. Light companies and grenadier companies had, in addition, a bugle horn and grenade, respectively, on the rosette. The feathers of the bonnet were fitted over a wire frame with the tails hanging on the right side. The 42nd did not have tails but flats of uncurled feathers. Officers' bonnets were always much fuller, taller and had more feathers than those of the men.

Officers' sporrans had now become more decorative, many having the tops and frames to the purse worked with thistle motifs and crown with regimental number and honours. Those of the rank and file continued to be plain white goats' hair with black tassels. On active service the sporran was not worn by the rank and file.

Officers' equipment included a cross-belt, worn over the right shoulder, which suspended the broadsword on the left hip and the dirk was suspended on the right front from a black leather waist-belt. The rank and file wore the standard infantry equipment, consisting of a pair of cross-belts in white buff leather supporting the ammunition pouch in black leather on the right hip and the bayonet on the left. The bayonet cross-belt was joined on the chest with a regimental-pattern belt plate while adjustment to the ammunition pouch belt was by means of brass buckles fitted to the belt just before it fastened to the ammunition pouch. The canvas knapsack which had been introduced in 1798 in place of a cow-hide one, was usually painted in the facing colour of the regiment with number in the centre but in about 1805 they were ordered to be painted black and the regimental number, or number and title, to be painted in white. For instance the 42nd (Royal Highlanders) painted the knapsack with '42 R.H.'. Marching-order equipment was completed by a white canvas haversack, slung on the left hip by a strap over the right shoulder, and a wood canteen on the right hip, also slung by a strap. On active service, however, the water canteen was slung on the left hip on top of the haversack to give easier access to the ammunition pouch. Sergeants of battalion companies wore only one cross-belt over the right shoulder – suspending the broad sword on the left hip as they carried the spontoon (halberd) and no musket – but sergeants of light and grenadier companies, being armed with the musket, wore the same equipment as privates.

In 1807, the 71st returned home from their captivity in Buenos Aires and had nothing but South American dress. Colonel Pack applied to the Adjutant General's office to be allowed to adopt tartan pantaloons for a temporary period as these could be supplied quicker so that the men on arrival in England could be issued with uniform clothing. The Adjutant General replied that the commander-in-chief agreed.

The 71st embarked for the Peninsula in 1808 wearing tartan pantaloons and in 1809 an inspection report found the 2nd Battalion wearing them also.

General F. Dundas received a letter from Horse Guards informing him that the 71st was now to consider itself a light-infantry regiment and to be armed and dressed as such. This removal of the 71st from the Highland establishment was followed on 7 April by the removal of six more Highland regiments – 72nd, 73rd, 74th, 75th, 91st and 94th. The reason for this move was explained in a Horse Guards' memorandum.

As the population of the Highlands of Scotland is found to be insufficient to supply recruits for the whole of the Highland Corps on the establishment of His Majesty's army, and as some of these corps laying aside their distinguishing dress, which is objectionable to the natives of South Britain, would, in a great measure, tend to facilitate the completing of their establishment, as it would be an inducement to the men of the English militia to extend their services in greater numbers to those regiments . . .

The regiments that remained on the Highland establishment were the 42nd (Royal Highlanders), 78th (Ross-shire Buffs), 79th (Cameron Highlanders) – whom one is tempted to suspect the Horse Guards took a wide berth of after Alan Cameron's reply of 1804 – 92nd (Gordon Highlanders) and, for some unaccountable reason, the youngest Highland regiment, the 93rd (Sutherland Highlanders).

During the Peninsular War, the war in America and the Waterloo campaign, the uniform of the Highland soldier did not change to any great extent. Highland regiments had adopted half hose and socks with short grey gaiters for active service in 1804. In 1808, the queue was abolished and the hair ordered to be cut short at the neck. The collar of the coat was made higher in 1808 and the sporran and belted plaid were discontinued for active service, the latter being replaced by the small kilt in about 1804. For some time previous, the belted plaid had been getting smaller and of a more decorative nature, falling down to just about hip level instead of to the bottom of the kilt. Officers of Highland regiments wore 'grey pantaloons and black gaiters' in place of the kilt and were noted in the Peninsula wearing pantaloons with boots or trousers with black or grey gaiters as did ordinary infantry officers; but the rest of their uniform was of Highland pattern. When pantaloons were worn, the plaid was tied across the body and pinned on the left shoulder, falling down to the hip.

As can be imagined, Highland uniform was a complete novelty to some of Britain's allies in the Peninsula and later during the Waterloo compaign. In August 1815, the Emperor of Russia, then residing at the Elysée Palace in Paris, expressed a desire to see the dress and accoutrements of the Highlanders (plate 16). Accordingly a sergeant, private and piper of the 42nd, 79th and 92nd were sent to the palace to perform various drills, including the 'manual and platoon exercises' in front of the Emperor. Sergeant Thomas Campbell of the 79th recounts that the Emperor was 'greatly pleased' and went on to add:

As soon as I stepped to the front, I was surrounded by the astonished nobility, and the Emperor commenced his inspection and questions as follows. First he examined my appointments and drew my sword; inquired if I could perform any exercise with the weapon, which I told him I could not, and at the same time Lord Cathcart made a remark that it was a deficiency in the British army he had never taken into consideration before.

Naturally the question of what a Highlander wore beneath his kilt came up and Thomas Campbell explains how the Emperor satisfied his curiosity:

Second, he examined my hose, gaiters, legs and pinched my skin, thinking I wore something under my kilt, and had the curiosity to lift my kilt to my navel, so that he might not be deceived.

After Waterloo, and the declaration of a general peace in Europe, there was a general trend to make uniforms more elaborate and more elegantly and richly adorned. When George, the Prince Regent, became George IV in 1820, he did much to further the increased elegance of military dress and two years after his accession the first general dress regulations were issued, which dealt with the dress to be worn by officers. The regulations described the senior regiment of each part of the army, which led to the rest of the Highland regiments attempting to adopt the treasured red hackle of the 42nd.

Other ranks' dress was not or never would be covered by dress regulations for the army (although the Royal Artillery and Royal Engineers in their separate regulations touched on them briefly). The following extracts from

PLATE 16 *Grenadiers of the 42nd and 92nd Highlanders, 1812 (from the* Costumes of the British Army *drawn by C. Hamilton Smith – Wrapper no 5 published September 1812).*

Dress Regulations 1822 describe what *should* have been worn.

The 'jacket' as it was called, had a 3in deep Prussian collar with a loop of lace and button on each side. Plate 17 shows the jacket of the 92nd which, although dating from c 1816, shows the style as described in the regulations of 1822. The slash flaps behind were decorated with four

loops and buttons and the white lined skirts and turnbacks were held by a regimental ornament.

The facing colours of the regiments in 1822 were: 42nd – blue; 78th – buff; 79th – dark green; 92nd – yellow; and 93rd – yellow. The lace colours and colour of the buttons were: 42nd – gold; 78th – gold; 79th – gold; 92nd – silver; and 93rd – silver.

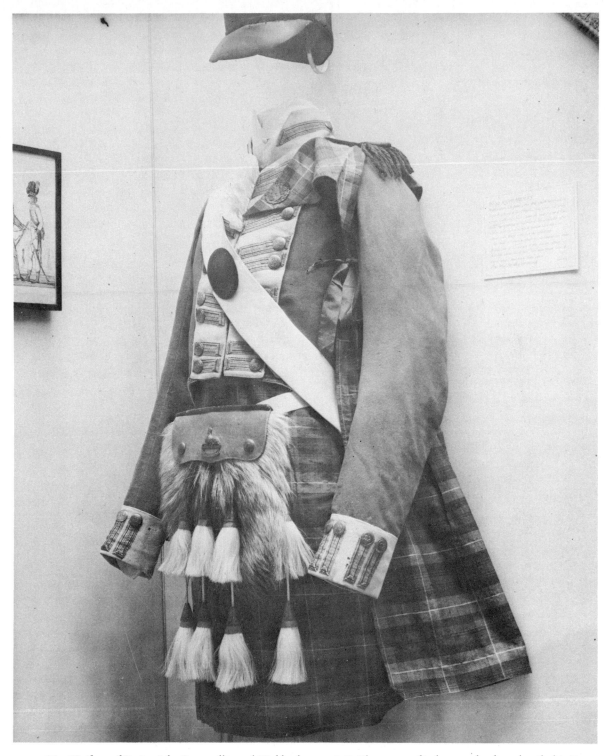

PLATE 17 *Uniform of Ensign John Bramwell, 92nd Highlanders, c 1816. The pattern of jacket was that later described in* Dress Regulations, *1822. Note that the epaulette and cross-belt plate are represented by black items: the real ones would have been silver.*

Epaulettes – With rounded straps two inches and a half wide, five inches and a half long, double bullion crescent, and single beading; two rows bright bullion, outer row three inches long; worn only by field officers, with the distinguishing badges of rank . . . Field officers wear both epaulettes and wings.

Badges of rank were: colonel, crown and star on the strap; lt-colonel, crown on the strap; major, star on the strap.

Wings – a pair; upper straps corresponding with straps of epaulettes, the lower, or wing part of the straps, of scarlet cloth, with embroidery; two rows of bullions, outer row about one inch and a quarter long; embroidered thistles on the straps – grenadier officers have grenades, and light infantry officers have bugles, above the thistles.

Waistcoat – scarlet, braided with gold. In regiments not authorised to wear lace, the waistcoat is to be plain.

Plaid and 'kelt' and hose and gaiters were described as 'according to Highland costume'.

Bonnet – cocked and feathered, about twelve inches deep; skull of tartan plaid, ornamented with six black ostrich feathers: a rosette, with regimental button, on the left side.

Feather – red vulture, twelve inches long.

The above items were worn in full dress. In the order 'Dress', the only difference was that blue-grey trousers with $^3/_4$in-wide gold-lace stripes, edged with scarlet cloth down the outside seams of each leg, were worn.

The 'undress' uniform differed in that the jacket was worn buttoned across and an undress cocked bonnet with small feather in front was worn. The dirk, in this order of dress, was worn on the left side.

The 'Regimental Staff' differed in that their jackets were single-breasted and a black feather was worn by the 'Surgeon and his Assistant'. The sash was not worn and a black leather sword-belt was worn under the coat.

Two items mentioned in *Dress Regulations* were the subjects of memorandums from the Horse Guards. The 'Red Vulture Feather' stated one, 'prescribed by the recent Regulations is intended to be used exclusively by the Fourty-Second Regiment'. In October 1822, the scarlet waistcoat was abolished and the old waistcoat, which was white, continued. The memorandum also added that 'white kerseymere pantaloons as worn by the infantry' were to be adopted by officers when the kilt was not worn.

George IV restored to two regiments certain Highland distinctions taken from them in 1809 but the kilt, the most Highland of all, was withheld and the regiments became non-kilted regiments. The 91st were restored only the title Argyllshire, while the 72nd received the Highland dress and trews in Prince Charles Edward Stewart tartan.

In 1829, lapels on officers' coatees were abolished and made to fasten across at all times, retaining the two rows of buttons. The cuffs of both officers and other ranks were altered from the round pattern with lace loops and buttons to a plain round cuff in the regimental facing colour with a scarlet slashed flap ornamented with four buttons. Between 1822 and 1830, battalion company officers of all Highland regiments had worn the wing flank-company-pattern epaulettes. In 1826, blue-grey trousers were ordered for winter wear and the lace was removed from officers' trousers; in 1828 a blue frock coat was introduced for officers as undress wear.

The undress bonnet mentioned in the 1822 regulations was abolished in 1829 and Highland regiments ordered to conform to the pattern laid down for the infantry but, in place of the band in the facing colour, they were permitted the band in 'the tartan of the regiment'.

Non-kilted regiments   1751–1830

The four Scottish regiments, dressed and accoutred as ordinary infantry in 1751 were the 1st or Royal Regiment, 21st or Royal North British Fuziliers, 25th or Edinburgh Regiment and 26th or Cameronians. The royal warrant of 1751 singled out only two for such special distinctions as the form of badges on colours and grenadier caps – the 1st and 21st.

The 1st had been raised in 1633 as Sir John Hepburne's Regiment, changing title in 1684 to the Royal Regiment of Foot and in 1751 to the 1st or Royal Regiment. In 1812, they became the 1st or Royal Scots, reverting to their 1751 title in 1821. This they retained until 1871 before becoming the 1st or the Royal Scots.

The 21st were raised in 1678 as the Earl of Mar's Regiment changing to the Royal Scotch Fuziliers in 1685 and to the 21st or Scotch Fusiliers in 1688. In 1707, they became the 21st or North British Fusiliers, adding 'Royal' in 1712.

The 25th were raised in 1698 as the Earl of Leven's Regiment, changing almost immediately to Leven's or the Edinburgh Regiment. In 1751 they became the 25th or the Edinburgh Regiment but in 1782 became the 25th

FIGURE 5 (Left) *private, 26th Regiment, 1742;* (right) *officer, 1st Foot, 1792.*

FIGURE 6 (Left) *private, 3rd Foot Guards, 1815*; (right) *officer, 73rd Foot, 1814.*

or Sussex Regiment, a title they retained until 1805 when they resumed their connection with Scotland, being styled the 25th or the King's Own Borderers.

The 26th was raised in 1689 as the Cameronians, a title retained until conversion to rifles in 1881. The typical appearance of an infantryman of 1742 is shown in fig 5 (left).

All four non-kilted Scottish regiments, augmented in 1794 by the raising of the 90th Perthshire Volunteers (Light Infantry), adhered strictly – except for buttons and regimental tape and lace – to the uniforms of the rest of the line, wearing the tricorn and then the shako in 1800. They wore, with their own distinctive facings colours, the coat with slope-away front and, from 1796, the single-breasted short-tailed coat. When the shako was adopted in 1800, the 1st and 25th were allowed to bear the number and device on the plate, in addition to the standard pattern of decoration. In 1812, when a new-pattern shako was ordered, this distinction was continued by a Horse Guards' circular of 14 February 1812, which stated that badges or other distinctions permitted for certain infantry regiments were to be worn on the 'appointments' and on the shako plate.

The 21st, who were permitted to bear the thistle appears, however, from surviving examples to have only placed the numeral '21' beneath the cipher on their cap plates. Hawkes, the well-known military tailors, have designs of special patterns of shako plates adopted in 1800. That of the 21st Foot, dated August 1800, shows that the plate bore the number 'XXI' on the left of the lion and 'Regt.' on the right.

All regiments wore the typical infantry-pattern coat, officers having faced lapels until 1829 and other ranks and officers having the round cuff with button-loops until the same year, when the slashed flap with buttons was introduced.

In 1809, the number of non-kilted Scottish regiments was increased when the 71st, 72nd, 73rd, 74th, 91st and 94th were deprived of the kilt and ordered to be dressed as line infantry, excepting the 71st who were transferred to light infantry. (The 73rd, given the number in India in 1786 and formed into a separate corps, rather than face disbandment – as the 2nd Battalion of the 42nd – did not wear the Highland dress and their inclusion in the War Office memorandum is a well-known official mistake [fig 6].)

The 71st, however, although not kilted, managed to fight successfully against removal from the Highland establishment. Having been informed from Horse Guards in March 1809 that they were to transfer to the light infantry, the 71st, although adopting light-infantry drill and muskets, continued to be dressed in trews and bonnets. On 31 January 1810, the commanding officer was advised by letter from Horse Guards that there appeared to have been a misconception regarding the 71st, who, although ordered to be dressed as light infantry, continued to wear trews in tartan and bonnets as if Highlanders.

Lt-Colonel Pack was quick to reply stating:

> I did not think it possible any misconception could exist as to the 71st being no longer considered a Highland Regiment, having myself understood from His Royal Highness the Duke of York and the present Commander-in-Chief that on becoming Light Infantry the Corps was to be put as to Colonel's allowances, clothing and appointments exactly on the same establishment as English Regiments of the Line, being only allowed to retain our name and such characteristics of the Old Corps as were in no way objectionable and out of which in point of esprit much good and no possible harm could arise; it was under this impression that the Bonnet cocked as a Regulation Cap was submitted to the Horse Guards for approbation and was sealed by the Adjutant General for our use.

Colonel Pack went on to 'entreat' that the regiment should be allowed to retain the cocked bonnet, the pipes and to dress their pipers in the 'Highland garb'.

The Adjutant General replied on 12 April that there was 'no objection to the 71st being denominated Highland Light Infantry' and that pipes and Highland garb were to be permitted for the pipers and the cocked bonnet 'lately approved' was to continue in use. The 71st were therefore dressed as light infantry with red coats with wing epaulettes and grey trousers and the bonnet 'cocked as a Light Infantry Cap'. Officers, however, seem to have given up the diced band at an early date and did not have dicing on the shako until 1862.

In 1823, the 91st were restyled Argyllshire – but with no change in dress – while the 72nd were permitted to dress as Highlanders but with the trews in place of the kilt and at the same time to adopt the title 72nd or the Duke of Albany's Own.

The only non-kilted Highland regiments wearing trews in 1830 were the 72nd and the 71st, who although termed Highland wore grey but kept their association with the Highlands in the form of their bonnet.

Chapter 3 Infantry
1830–1881

Kilted Regiments   1830–1855

Drastic changes were made in the army in 1830 by order of the new King, William IV. Henceforth, all regular regiments would adopt gold lace and gilt buttons for the officers, silver being reserved for militia and volunteers. This order affected the 92nd and 93rd, both of which wore silver lace, the former with a blue-black worm running through which was retained in the gold lace.

In 1830, Highland regiments were ordered to carry the basket-hilt sword with steel basket in place of the brass basket used from the end of the eighteenth century and on 13 April 1830 an order from the Adjutant General's office authorised trews in the regimental tartan for all occasions when the kilt was not worn. Because of the various changes – some small, others major – which had occurred since 1822, the new *Dress Regulations* were issued in 1831. The following shows the items that had changed since 1822.

The jacket according to the new regulations was double-breasted with two rows of ten buttons, a Prussian collar with two bars of lace and buttons, round cuffs in the regimental colour and a slashed flap in scarlet with four buttons and laced loops on the cuff and skirts. The bonnet increased in height from 12in to 14in and a 'regimental button or badge' was authorised for the rosette on the left side. The vulture feather, however, decreased from 12in

in 1822 to 8in. The *'Belted Plaid, Kilt, Purse, Hose, Garters, Shoes* and *Buckles'* were 'according to Highland costume and to established regimental patterns'.

The *'Scarf'* worn by Highland officers when not wearing the kilt was mentioned as being 'according to regimental pattern, to be worn with the red jacket on occasions when the kilt is not worn'. When the scarf was worn, the crimson sash was not.

Two other items mentioned were the frock coat and the forage cap, the latter being 'of blue cloth, with a band and welt of regimental Tartan, and black leather peak'. The shell jacket was scarlet, as worn by the infantry. The 72nd was noted as wearing trews on all occasions but otherwise officers were dressed in the normal Highland manner.

Field officers were ordered to wear a waist-belt in place of the buff shoulder-belt and decorative regimental-pattern plate and to have brass scabbards for their swords, although this latter part of the order did not apply to Highland regiments, whose field officers at this time still retained the broadsword in a steel scabbard.

The rank and file retained the same uniform and equipment as previously and the supply of clothing for 'Regiments wearing Highland Clothing' was regulated as:

. . . annually, for Regiments wearing the kilt:
A coat, a waistcoat with sleeves and a pair of shoes. 15/–

PLATE 18   *92nd Highlanders on the march (from a coloured lithograph by Lynch and Hayes, published by Spooner, 1833). Note the foul-weather covers worn over the bonnets.*

in money to each Sergeant and 7/9 to each man of all other ranks, towards the provision of Highland articles hereafter established as part of the soldier's necessaries.

In regiments wearing trews it was '13/6 to each Sergeant and 6/– to other ranks'. Necessaries were regulated as:

> Bonnet, complete with drooping feathers, hackle, cockade and oilskin cover. Plaid, kilt, fatigue trousers, three pairs hose garters and rosettes, shoes and buckles, knee cap, purse and belt.

There were in addition, shirts, stocks, brushes of various sorts, knapsack with straps, blacking, soap etc. A knee pad was provided to protect the kilted soldier when kneeling and was not provided for regiments wearing trousers or trews.

New *Dress Regulations* were issued in 1834 and officers' forage caps were altered and the band made of regimental

bonnet tartan with an embroidered thistle with regimental number below, or badge for those regiments entitled.

In 1836 there were a number of changes affecting officers and other ranks. A general order of 17 March introduced a new pattern of Highland jacket having 'each skirt 9 inches long, $6^1/_4$ inches at the bottom and $7^1/_4$ inches at the top, and so cut as to rest on the hips, and the turnbacks not seen in front'.

In October of the same year, regimental-pattern tape was abolished, plain white taking its place. Sergeants were ordered a double-breasted jacket with brass buttons and devoid of tape. The clothing for the year 1838 was ordered to be prepared according to the new regulations.

In 1834, the bonnet for officers was 13in, reverting to 14in in 1846, the year of a new issue of *Dress Regulations* but it increased the following year to 16in. In 1845, sergeants' sashes were ordered to be without the central strips of regimental facing colour and to be 'National

FIGURE 7 *Cross-belt plates:* (top, left to right) *Black Watch (42nd and 73rd) 1881 onwards; 74th Foot, 1817–20; 90th Foot, 1830–45.* (bottom, left to right) *Highland Light Infantry (71st and 74th), 1881–1957; 72nd Foot, 1825–55; 92nd Foot, 1800.*

crimson colour throughout' and to be reduced in width to 2¹/₂in.

Other ranks' Highland uniform is shown in plate 18, one of the series of prints by M. A. Hayes and J. H. Lynch. The regiment depicted is the 92nd on the march, with the bonnets in oilskin cover, skirmishers in front and on the flanks. The 92nd had the added distinction, ordered in 1822, of the battalion company wearing light and the grenadier company pattern wing epaulettes. The bonnet for battalion and light companies was 12in high, while that of the grenadier companies was 14in high. All regiments, except the 42nd, wore a white hackle, the individual distinction between light and grenadier companies having been given up in 1829. Officers of the battalion companies of the 92nd, however, did not wear 'wings'. A sergeant of the 92nd is shown (fig 7) in plate 19 wearing the single cross-belt with plate to suspend the broadsword and the regimental-pattern sporran with brass-rimmed

top, adopted about 1830 (fig 8). In place of the badge in the centre on the sergeant's sporran, other ranks had an additional tassel.

An officer of the 79th Highlanders in the uniform of the period is shown in plate 20.

New *Dress Regulations* were issued in 1846, which with minor variations describe the uniform worn by officers in the Crimean War of 1854–6 – before the radical changes of 1855 and 1856 to the uniforms of the entire army. The jacket was as described in the regulations of 1830 (see p 50) and the epaulettes and wings were according to regulations for infantry of the line. Highland regiments were ordered to have in addition, on the strap of the epaulette, a thistle and to substitute the thistle for the bugle or grenade on the plate of the 'wings'.

The frock coat was blue and single-breasted with eight buttons down the front, a Prussian collar and two buttons on each cuff. The shoulder straps were in blue cloth, edged round in regimental-pattern lace, with a metal crescent at the end (fig 9). Highland regiments were ordered to have the thistle within the crescent.

The forage cap, worn with the frock coat or the scarlet shell jacket, was in blue cloth,

> with a red seam round the crown; band of regimental bonnet Tartan; an embroidered thistle, with the number of the regiment on the lower part of it, (except in the 42nd Regiment, where the badge of St. Andrew is substituted for the number); black leather peak, and chin strap.

FIGURE 8 *Purse or sporran of 92nd Foot, 1848 (from a drawing in the pattern book of Wilkinson & Son).*

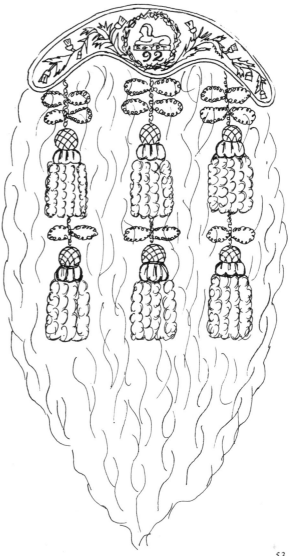

PLATE 19 *Sergeant in full dress, 92nd Highlanders, c 1850. Note the regimental-pattern cross-belt plate and sporran.*

PLATE 20   *Officer, flank company 79th, 1840. In the background is a private of the regiment.*

Regimental staff were not required to wear the plaid or kilt and wore the same uniform as other officers but with black feather for the surgeon and without the sash. A waist-belt with slings was worn under the jacket for the sword. Regimental staff officers of Highland regiments wore the bonnet and trews, unlike infantry staff officers who wore a cocked hat.

In 1848, the single-breasted frock coat was ordered to be discontinued and the scarlet shell jacket adopted 'with facings but without lace or other ornament to be worn without sash in quarters, on fatigues or orderly duties, and at drill or on parade when the men happened to be dressed in the same manner'. With the shell jacket, a black leather belt with slings suspended the sword and dirk. Full-dress uniform was to be worn at mess in spite of the repeated efforts of officers to have the shell jacket adopted for wear in the mess. The forage cap was worn with the shell jacket.

On 7 July 1851, an order was issued which stated that all kilted regiments were to discontinue wearing the undress bonnet, or forage cap, and to wear instead a glengarry bonnet 'with Regimental band or border the same as on the bonnet'. Other Highland regiments were to wear the forage cap 'of the same form as the rest of the Infantry, with the Regimental National band or border'.

The pork-pie cap, worn in undress by the infantry, was often referred to as a 'Kilmarnock' but is not to be confused with the later head-dress of that name adopted by Lowland regiments in 1904. The cap took its name from the Kilmarnock makers, who were very large suppliers to the army.

Kilted regiments wearing the glengarry placed a badge on the left side above the band of dicing which had a 'V' at the back and two black tapes for adjusting to the head.

An order of 8 July 1852 reintroduced the frock coat for officers but only for wear in the vicinity of quarters and never with troops on parade. The new garment was double-breasted. In the same year, a new pattern of forage cap with a smaller top was introduced for officers. A diced band continued to be a feature of the cap for Highland regiments, except in the case of the 42nd who wore one of the regimental or government tartan.

The equipment of the British infantryman was altered in 1852 by the removal of the bayonet cross-belt and the elaborate plate that fastened it. In its place, a waist-belt was issued with bayonet frog and an extra black ammunition pouch was worn on the right front, fitted to the belt. The waist-belt had been used 'unofficially' by some regiments, especially light infantry, who found that at the run the two belts allowed the pouch and bayonet to bang up and down and to become unpositioned. A waist-belt was used to keep the belts and pouch in place. With the new issue of the waist-belt, a smaller ammunition pouch was ordered to be fitted to the existing cross-belt.

In 1854, pipers were given official sanction – but not for all regiments and certainly not for any Lowland regiments. Prior to this date pipers had been maintained by regiments at the officers' expense but in 1854 one pipe major at 1s 10d per day and five pipers at 1s 1d per day were authorised.

A good idea of Highland military uniform for kilted regiments prior to the drastic changes of 1855 are given in plate 21, a photograph of a group of officers of the 42nd by Roger Fenton, and plate 22, a photograph by Robertson of a group of officers, NCOs and men of the 93rd at Scutari.

The officer on the left in the Fenton photograph is wearing full dress but with the forage cap with St Andrew badge in place of the bonnet. The other three officers are all wearing various forms of 'unofficial' uniform which always seemed to creep into use on active service. All are wearing tartan trews and – with the exception of the officer in the rather strange tartan jacket – the scarlet shell jacket, black waist-belt and slings and swords.

The Robertson photograph shows two officers, the one on the left wearing the scarlet shell jacket, trews and forage cap and the other wearing full-dress coat with epaulettes, shoulder-belt and sash, kilt, hose, gaiters and sporran. The

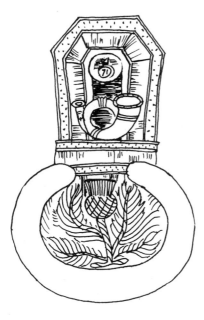

FIGURE 9   *Officer's frock-coat epaulette, c 1854.*

other ranks wear the short-tailed Highland-pattern coat, with the plain white-taped button-loops on the chest and wing epaulettes with worsted half-moon ends. All wear the kilt, sporran, hose and gaiters as well as the 1852 improved equipment with waist-belt. On the right of the picture are three men – one corporal and two privates – in the white-sleeved waistcoat and the glengarry with diced border. The corporal's rank stripes were red on the white jacket (white on the red full-dress coat). The corporal also wears a badger-head sporran.

Kilted regiments   1855–1881

The reforms in the design of uniforms appeared in a new edition of *Dress Regulations* in 1855. This, as previously,

described only the dress to be worn by officers but the spread of photography, and notably the series of Crimean heroes taken at Queen Victoria's suggestion, give details of the new uniform worn by the rank and file of the Highland regiments, amongst others.

The new 'jacket', as it was still termed, was in fact a doublet for Scottish regiments. It was scarlet and double-breasted with the collar, cuffs and lapels in the facing colour. The lapels were made to be worn open in some cases or completely buttoned over. The slashed-flap cuff was retained but epaulettes abolished in favour of twisted gold-corn shoulder-straps. Ranking was now borne on the collar and the lower half of the jacket below the waist was a complete departure from any known military fashion. 'Inverness skirts', as they were termed, were part of Highland jackets. These flaps in scarlet, both at the front and behind, were decorated with button loops and buttons. At the back, between the Inverness skirts were smaller un-

PLATE 22   *Officer, NCOs and men of the 93rd at Scutari, 1855 (from an original photograph by Robertson). Notice new-pattern equipment with single cross-belt, the NCO's badger-head sporran and the glengarry worn with the white-sleeved waistcoat.*

decorated skirt flaps. Field officers had the added distinction of additional bands of gold lace on the sleeve, skirt flaps and Inverness skirts, as well as the collar.

With the abolition of the epaulette, rank badges were transferred to the collar. The new system was extremely complicated and relied on the use of only three types of rank badge to distinguish six ranks of officer. The following extract from the regulation explains how, by the combination of embroidered badges and rows of lace, rank was meant to be recognised:

> *Colonel,* a crown and star. *Lieutenant-Colonel,* a crown. *Major,* a star.
> The other Officers have half-inch lace round the top of the collar, one row of the same round the top of the cuff, and the following distinctions at each end of the collar: *Captain,* a crown and star. *Lieutenant,* a crown. *Ensign,* a star.

For Highland regiments – and this included the non-kilted – the button were 'gilt diamond shaped, bearing the number of the regiment surmounted by a crown'.

Highland regiments also managed to retain the white buff cross-belt, with its elaborate plate, for the sword. The illustration (plate 23) from Ackerman's *Costumes of the British Army (The New Series)* of the 42nd, published in February 1856, shows the uniform worn by an officer according to the new regulations – although the slashed flap on the cuff is shown as red, whereas it should of course be blue, the facing colour. As can be seen, no waist-belt was worn over the doublet, the dirk being suspended from a black leather belt worn under it. The rest of the uniform remained the same as pre-Crimea.

A colour sergeant – Gardener, who was later to win the Victoria Cross during the Indian Mutiny – and two privates of the 42nd are shown in plate 24, one of the photographs of Crimean heroes. They wear the new double-breasted doublet in red (sergeants, however had theirs in scarlet) with nine diamond-shaped brass buttons in each row on the front, in place of the round pewter buttons worn on the previous coats. The piping down the leading edge, around the Inverness skirts, cuffs and slash are white and the button-loops of the slash in white worsted braid. The epaulettes gave way to shoulder-straps in red, edged in white and bearing the regimental number. The rest of the uniform and equipment shown is the same as was worn before the Crimea. The waist-belt, introduced in 1852, had a regimental-pattern locket with the number in the centre and the title around the outer edge (plate 24). The sporran of the 42nd was in white hair with a leather

top and five tassels, the badge of St Andrew being placed on a small shield just below the top. The method of carrying the mess tin and rolled blanket on the knapsack is clearly shown, as is the regimental number in white on the knapsack itself. Another unusual feature of the new doublet was the small pocket, which contained percussion caps for the rifle, to the right of the fastening. An extra black leather pouch was worn on the right side of the belt but is not shown in this plate.

In the same series are two representations (plate 25) of pipers' dress: Piper Muir of the 42nd and Pipe-Major Macdonald of the 72nd (a non-kilted Highland regiment whose pipers did wear the kilt). The pipe-major wears the glengarry, but without dicing, and elaborate gold knots on the shoulder as well as 'gauntlet' cuffs, a feature of all Scottish Highland uniforms not introduced until 1868. The pipers of the 42nd wore the feather bonnet, which was retained after 1860 when other regiments put their pipers in the glengarry and the double-breasted doublet with slashed cuff. Another feature is the wing on the right shoulder. Both photographs also show the pipe banner.

In 1855, the double-breasted officers' frock coat is described. This now had the ranking on the collar and a simple twisted crimson cord on the shoulders to retain the cross-belt and sash. The cuffs in blue had a slashed flap in the same colour with three buttons and behind on the skirts a further slashed flap, 10in deep, had buttons.

The shell jacket was in scarlet cloth with a rounded collar and pointed cuffs in the facing colour. It was single-breasted and fastened with small buttons down the front at equal distances. There were also two buttons on the cuff. Field officers, as in the case of the frock coat, were the only ones to bear ranking on the collar.

The double-breasted doublet was replaced in 1856 by a single-breasted one and regiments who had the diamond-shaped button replaced it with a normal round pattern, as it had been found that the diamond shape caused excessive wear on the buttonholes. The new 'jacket' was described in the 1857 edition of *Dress Regulations* as being scarlet with 'eight buttons at equal distances, and a fly one and three-quarter inch wide, thus buttoning well over'. Otherwise the doublet was the same as previously.

The bonnet was 12in deep, 'cocked and feathered with six black ostrich feathers', but had the addition of a chin-strap.

Field officers were ordered to wear a waist-belt, and regimental officers the cross-belt. The other ranks still retained the glengarry and the white waistcoat with sleeves for drill and undress.

PLATE 23 *Officer, 42nd Highlanders, in the double-breasted tunic of 1856. Notice no waist-belt worn over the coat and ranking on the collar now that epaulettes had been abolished.*

While the uniforms described above continued to be worn both at home and at other stations, the Indian Mutiny had broken out, which necessitated the immediate despatch of troops to India. There were, as there had been previously, special regulations in force for 'Queen's Regiments' proceeding to India for a tour of duty. A War Office memorandum of 1857 stated that every soldier on his arrival in India was to be provided with four white jackets, one pair of English summer trousers, five pairs of white trousers, two checked shirts and a pair of braces. Any money available to the colonel from the necessaries was to be used to buy clothing suited to the climate but any surplus money was to be given to the soldier.

A great variety of dress, usually unofficial, was worn

PLATE 24   *Colour-Sergeant Gardener, Privates Mackenzie and Glen, 42nd Highlanders, in uniforms introduced in 1856. This plate, one of the series of Crimean heroes, shows the new tunic with Inverness skirts, diamond-shaped buttons and shoulder-straps in place of epaulettes.*

during the Indian Mutiny as the circumstances dictated and included khaki-dyed white clothing:

> 'Karkee' or dust colour . . . which before May 1857 was only seen across the Indus, was a sort of grey drab varying very much in tint but adopted by Frontier troops for their hill fighting being nearly the colour of the desert . . .

The variety of shades produced was enormous and often no two men from the same company were dressed in the same tint.

All the kilted Highland regiments were involved in India during the mutiny. The 42nd is recorded as being issued with wicker helmets in 1858. The Adjutant General had written on the subject to the President in Council suggesting that the shako which was worn with a white quilted cover be discontinued in India and

> . . . replaced by a light helmet-shaped cap made of wicker and covered with cotton cloth, wound around with a thick turban. The advantage is it protects the temples and sides of the head which no shako cover does . . . they would last a year and cost about two rupees.

The 78th's only concession to the climate appears to have been the use of a quilted bonnet-cover, the campaign being conducted in 'red woollen doublets and feather bonnets' and the normal kilt, sporran, hose and gaiters.

The 79th, which arrived at Calcutta on 27 November 1857 was sent 'up country as quickly as possible'. The men did not get their 'Indian outfit' so wore the doublet with green facings, kilt, sporran with patent-leather top and St Andrew badge, kilt, hose and gaiters. The bonnet was worn with a 'sun shade', a quilted cover, with peak and neck flap. An ex-soldier writing in 1902 recollects 'A quilted sunshade and light blue muslin puggarees were issued to wear with the glengarries.'

The 92nd also wore the red doublet and normal uniform with a quilted cover for the bonnet and grey hose but the 93rd appeared in brown Holland jackets with red collar, cuffs and shoulder-straps which bore the regimental number. The officers' jackets were made of alpaca but with the same colour collar and cuffs and twisted-cord shoulder-cords. A large quilted cover was issued to wear on the bonnet with peak and neck flap and the inside lining of the bonnet was removed, leaving the wire frame to make the head-dress cooler and lighter.

At the end of the Indian Mutiny, the various 'unofficial' uniforms – whites died with tea or tobacco juice and other dyes – were speedily discarded and whites and reds were

FIGURE 10 *Officer's waist-belt plate, 92nd Foot, c 1848 (from a drawing in the pattern book of Wilkinson & Son – later Wilkinson Sword Ltd).*

again the colour of the uniforms. Any lessons that had been learned about camouflage and the use of khaki were soon forgotten by the regular army and uniforms once again assumed the appearance of peace. Khaki had been all very well in the conditions of the mutiny but as a dress for the soldier it was considered unsmart, lacking in any source of personal or regimental pride and considered by the troops as little better than the garb worn by the native sweepers and stable hands.

Flank companies, or the light and grenadier companies, were abolished in 1862 and regiments divided into ten companies denoted by letters. Abroad, a battalion would be composed of ten service companies and two depot companies. Circular Memorandum no 38 from Horse Guards dated 30 May 1860 stated that men were not to be selected for any particular company and that 'officers commanding are to place such companies on the flanks as they from time to time deem most expedient'.

About 1859, the 42nd and 92nd changed their hose from red and white to red and black while the 79th changed to red and green. In 1860, pipers of all Highland regiments, as well as those Lowland regiments and non-kilted regiments allowed them, changed their doublets from red to green and adopted a plain glengarry without dicing, usually topped by a blackcock's feather. The 42nd, however, preferred to maintain its pipers in the bonnet. Those regiments who changed, however, still continued to draw the allowed number of bonnets for their pipers, relegating them to the band.

In 1861, the 42nd, 92nd and 93rd were accorded extra titles which became official. The 42nd became the Black

PLATE 25   *Pipe-Major MacDonald of 72nd Highlanders, 1856. Notice the early use of the gauntlet cuff (not introduced into Scottish uniform until 1868), the twisted shoulder cords and glengarry.*

Watch, the 92nd, the Gordon Highlanders and the 93rd, the Sutherland Highlanders.

A representative view of Highland uniform is shown in plate 26, which depicts officers, colour sergeants, privates, piper and pioneers of the 92nd in 1861.

In 1866, regimental-pattern bugler's lace was abolished and white lace with small red crown made universal. In 1868, all Highland regiments discontinued the slashed-flap cuff and adopted the gauntlet cuff with three white worsted braid loops and buttons for rank and file and gold braid replacing the white for officers. An innovation for officers was the introduction of the blue frogged patrol jacket as shown in plate 28. This, the same as worn by infantry officers, was made of blue cloth, edged in black mohair lace and frogged with four loops, bars and olivets on the front in black. It was worn with the forage cap and trews and the sword worn on the belt under the jacket.

Plate 27 shows an officer of the 78th with the gauntlet cuff. The officer is wearing the plaid with regimental-pattern brooch, gold-embroidered dirk belt and full-dress sporran with gilt metal top, goat hair and gold-cord tassels. The crown on the collar and the single line of lace on the cuff show the officer to be a lieutenant.

In 1870, a section of the 93rd Foot formed a guard of honour for Queen Victoria at Ballater. The Queen noticed that, as a result of wind and rain, the rough wet tartan had scratched and cut the soldiers' legs. Accordingly the Queen directed that in future all Highland regiments should be supplied with soft tartan in place of the 'hard' tartan that had always previously been supplied.

In the same year 'valise' equipment was introduced in place of the knapsack equipment with the cross-belt for the ammunition pouch but, as with all new patterns, it took time to be issued to all regiments. The new equipment consisted of a waist-belt with bayonet frog on the left hip and two white braces attached to the belt at the front, passing over the shoulders and crossing at the back before passing under the arms and fastening back to the brace about 6in above the belt. The valise was carried on the top of the buttocks, strapped to the braces with the rolled greatcoat and mess tin above – the latter between the valise and greatcoat. When the bonnet was worn, the glengarry was tucked into the straps of the greatcoat. The pouches of the new equipment were black – except for the regiments of Foot Guards and the 29th Foot – and continued to be so until the early 1880s.

In 1870, the rank of ensign was replaced by sub-lieutenant and the following year, the time-honoured tradition of purchase of commissions was abolished. In the

following year, the dull brick red – or 'madder red' as it was known – of the rank and file doublets below sergeants were changed to scarlet. At the same time the bands of infantry regiments, who had since pre-Crimea days been dressed in white, adopted the scarlet doublet. In 1873, the shoulder-straps of the doublets were changed to the regimental facing colour and the embroidered numerals of the regiment changed to white metal ones. Three years later, regimental-pattern brass buttons were abolished for all except officers, who wore gilt, and a 'universal' pattern was adopted. This button bore on it the royal arms. At the same time, to avoid confusion, collar badges were introduced for each regiment.

In 1873, by express command of Queen Victoria, the 79th was in future to be styled the 79th Queen's Own Cameron Highlanders and to alter its facings from green to the blue of royal regiments. At the same time they were granted the special badge of the thistle, ensigned with the Imperial crown. The badge, it was stated, 'being the badge of Scotland as sanctioned by Queen Anne in 1707 on the confirmation of the Act of Union of the two kingdoms'. In the same year a scarlet frock tunic was introduced for undress wear. In the Highland regiments this had the familiar gauntlet cuffs but did not have Inverness skirts – the front edges sloped away and the pocket flaps each side below the waist had three white worsted braid loops and buttons.

A further edition of *Dress Regulations* was issued in 1874. Since the Crimea, they had appeared at remarkably frequent intervals: 1855, 1857, 1861, 1864 and 1872. The new regulations described the 'Dress Jacket' as scarlet cloth, single-breasted and with collar and cuff laced according to rank. The main departure from the previous regulations was the first mention of mess dress.

The mess waistcoat was to be 'as for Infantry of the line or of Regimental tartan'. The 92nd was again authorised its special braid. The waistcoat was worn under the open shell jacket which was in scarlet cloth with 'gold braid edging all round, including top and bottom of collar'. Twisted gold shoulder-cords were worn and the front had a row of 'gilt studs and hooks and eyes down the front'. It had pointed cuffs decorated with Austrian knots.

The glengarry was authorised in place of the forage cap for kilted Highland regiments and was described as:

Blue cloth of pattern similar to that worn by the men. Plain in the 42d and 79th, diced in the 78th, 92d and 93d regiments. Bottom of cap bound with black silk. Badges to be worn on the left side. 42d a *star* cross of St Andrew

PLATE 26 *Officers, NCOs, men, piper, drummer and pioneer of the Depot Company, 92nd Highlanders, 1861. Notice the forage cap worn by the officers and the extra bands of lace on the cuffs and skirts to denote rank.*

in silver or white metal, and on the cross, in gold or gilt metal, a circle, with the motto 'Nemo me impune lacessit'. The circle enclosed by a wreath of thistles. Number of the regiment in silver in the centre of circle. Above the circle, the crown, below the sphinx, both in gold . . .

79th. St Andrew and Cross within a wreath of thistles.

92d. The crest of the Marquis of Huntley above the number of the regiment. The crest encircled by a wreath of ivy.

93d. Within a garter the number of the Regiment and on the garter the words 'Sutherland Highlanders'. The garter surrounded without and within by a wreath of thistles.

All the badges, except for that of the 42nd were in white metal.

Plate 29 shows a field officer of the 79th in 1876 and the

bars of lace and braid can clearly be seen on the cuff and skirt-flaps. This also shows the saddlecloth of a field officer in the face colour, edged in lace and bearing, on the hind part, the badge of rank.

In about 1870, a white helmet had been introduced for wear on foreign stations and in India in place of the bonnet. For dress wear, it was crowned with a gilt or brass spike and had gilt or brass chin-chains. The 42nd wore a small red hackle in the left side of the puggaree – the tightly wound linen band that encircled the helmet.

In 1877 Colonel Stanley's committee on the army recommended that a closer connection should be made between the line battalions of a brigade and the militia of a sub-district. This could best be accomplished by

their being treated as one regiment, such regiment bearing a Territorial designation; the Line Battalions being the 1st and 2nd; the Militia Battalions the 3rd and

PLATE 27 *Officer, 78th Highlanders, c 1870. This plate shows the typical appearance of a Highland regimental officer after the introduction of the gauntlet cuff in 1868.*

4th etc., of such Territorial regiment; the Depot being common to all, and being the last battalion of the series.

In 1881, the Ellice Committee on the formation of Territorial regiments made the following suggestion as regards the linking of the Highland regiments.

42nd and 79th. The Black Watch and Cameron Royal Highland Regiment (Queen's Own).
92nd and 93d. The Gordon and Sutherland Highland Regiment.

The 78th, a kilted regiment was combined with the 71st, a light-infantry regiment wearing trews, as the Inverness and Ross Regiment (Highland Light Infantry).

General Order 41 of 1 May 1881 rearranged the proposed links.

42nd and 73rd. The Royal Highlanders (Black Watch).
79th. The Queen's Own Cameron Highlanders.
91st and 93rd. The Sutherland and Argyll Highlanders (Princess Louise's).
75th and 92nd. The Gordon Highlanders.

General Order 70 of 1 July 1881 amended some of the new regimental titles: the 42nd and 73rd became the Black Watch (Royal Highlanders), the 72nd and 78th, the Seaforth Highlanders (the Ross-shire Buffs) and the 91st and 93rd assumed the title Princess Louise's (Sutherland and Argyll Highlanders). In 1882, Sutherland and Argyll was altered to Argyll and Sutherland.

PLATE 28 *Officer, NCOs and private, Gordon Highlanders (75th and 92nd), 1896, in various orders of dress. Notice the officer's patrol jacket with frogged front and the difference in sporrans between NCOs and private.*

PLATE 29 *Field officer, 79th Highlanders, 1876 (from an original watercolour by R. Simkin). Note the ranking worn on the saddlecloth which was in the regimental face colour and the breeches and boots in lieu of the kilt.*

Non-kilted regiments   1830–1855

The non-kilted regiments in 1830 who were on the High-land establishment were the 72nd, who wore the Highland uniform – except that trews replaced the kilt and officers wore the plaid scarf across the body at all times. The other regiment was the 71st, whose link – besides its numbering – was in the bonnet cocked like a light-infantry cap. The other regiments were the 1st, 25th, 26th and 90th and of those removed from the Highland establishment in 1809, only one, the 91st maintained a link by its title – Argyll-shire.

The 1st, 25th, 26th, 90th and 91st were dressed, equipped and accoutred as ordinary line infantry, nothing in their uniform being specially Scottish except for the badges some were entitled to bear. In order to follow the evolution of military dress, as it concerned these regi-ments, the various changes are listed below, space not permitting a fuller treatment in a book devoted to Scottish uniforms.

1830   Horse Guards circular of 27 July discontinued the cap lines worn on the bell-shaped shako. Feather shortened to 8in and a green ball-tuft adopted by light companies and light infantry. Bands adopt white coatees with collar cuffs and wing epaulettes of the facing colour. Gorgets abolished for officers. General Order 495 abolished silver lace for regular regiments, all in future to wear gold. Field officers adopt waist-belt, regimental officers retaining the cross-belt.

1832   Breeches discontinued.

1833   Red welt added to the outside seam of 'Oxford mixture' trousers.

1834   New forage cap adopted by officers.

1835   Ball-tufts introduced for all shakos in place of plume by Horse Guards circular 27 August. Peak and plate of grenadiers' bearskin caps discontinued.

1836   Regimental-pattern tape abolished for rank and file and plain white substituted. Sergeants wore a double-breasted coatee without lace on the chest (General Order 522 of 1836). The skirts of the coatee altered in cut. Flap opening on trousers altered to fly front.

1839   New pattern of bell-shaped shako with round plate surmounted by crown with number in the centre for rank and file.

1842   Chin-chain introduced on officers' shakos in place of scales. Bearskin cap discontinued for grenadiers.

1844   New pattern of shako adopted. Authorised 4 December 1843.

1845   Coloured stripe of the face colour in sergeants' sashes abolished. Crimson throughout (circular memorandum 6 August 1845).

1846   White trousers abolished for summer wear at home. Summer trousers of a lavender mixture adopted but altered to indigo blue in 1850.

1848   Blue frock coat with shoulder scales abolished for officers, scarlet shell jacket worn in its place. Imi-tation pocket flaps on the skirts of officers' coatees removed.

The uniform of the non-Highland Scottish regiments is shown in fig 11 *(left)*. This gives a good idea of the pre-Crimean uniforms.

The 26th at this period had a diced band – the authority of which was questioned in 1862 (see p 79) – on the forage caps of both officers and men (plate 30). The 72nd, until 1881, dressed as a Highland regiment except that the men wore trews and scarf of Prince Charles Edward Stewart tartan – a similar design to Royal Stewart. The 72nd will be only briefly mentioned as changes in uniform and so on conform with the changes in the other Highland regi-ments.

In 1834 came a number of changes in the uniform of the 71st. It had already adopted the bell-shaped shako with green ball-tuft and dicing for the other ranks. The officers had a band of black thistle-pattern lace in place of the dicing. All ranks wore black festoons and officers added cap lines. Both these distinctions were retained long after they had been abolished for the rest of the army. A letter of 21 February 1834 from Horse Guards stated that the King had been pleased to approve the resumption of the Highland 'tartan scarf' formerly in use by the 71st.

On 5 April the wearing of trews in tartan in place of 'trowsers of the description now worn' – Oxford mixture', adopted by Horse Guards circular memorandum of 10 February 1829 – was authorised and the regiment chose for both scarf and trews the Mackenzie tartan as worn by the 78th Highland Regiment and, until 1809, by the 71st.

The shako worn in about 1834 was of similar shape and dimensions as that worn by the infantry, except that in the 71st, officers had black thistle-pattern lace around the top and bottom and rank and file had a diced band around the bottom in white, red and green. Both officers and rank and file had plaited cap lines falling over the peak with floun-ders on the right side. Officers had lines which hooked to

FIGURE 11 (Left) *officer, 1st Foot, 1838;* (right) *private, 91st Foot, 1854.*

PLATE 30 *Officer, 26th Regiment, 1835, in frock coat and forage cap. Notice the regimental distinction of a diced band for the 26th.*

a button on the coatee but rank and file did not. The chin-strap was in black leather with a small buckle for adjustment.

The dimensions of the cap were the same as for the infantry of the line shako, introduced by a Horse Guards circular dated 2 July 1830. The body of the shako was of black beaver, 6in high and with a sunken glazed-leather top of 11in diameter. The top and bottom of the shako were bound with a band of black leather, connected by thinner side-straps stitched to the shako in a 'V' shape. For the 71st, however, the top and bottom bands were black thistle-pattern lace with possibly the side-straps of the same material, and the top and body of the shako were in cloth. In the centre of the top band of lace was a corded boss with a gilt metal thistle on it. Fitted behind the boss was a socket for the green ball in a brass thistle-holder. The badge was a stringed bugle horn, fitted in the centre above the flounders.

The rank and file 'bonnet' was blue cloth with the diced band, badge, flounders, ball in holder and a red tourrie or wool tuft, on the top. Unlike the shako, the bonnet was woven without seam and 'shrunk' on or cocked as a bell-top shako.

As light infantry, officers wore a chain and whistle on the cross-belt, as did sergeants, but this practice seems to have been given up in the 71st about 1836.

In 1836, the officers adopted the Highland-pattern jacket that was approved that year, having adopted the Highland-pattern coatee on 20 December 1834 after reverting to tartan trews and adopting the scarf. The 1836 coatee was as described (see p 52). In common with the rest of the infantry, regimental-pattern tape was abolished for rank and file in 1836 and sergeants wore a plain double-breasted coatee.

The service companies of the 71st proceeded to Canada in 1838 where, during the winter, pointed fur hats and long boots were worn with the greatcoat and cap by the rank and file. Officers wore fur-trimmed coats with black cord braiding and knots on the chest.

About 1841, the 71st adopted the French hunting-horn badge in place of the stringed bugle horn for the shako, shoulder-belt plate, buttons and epaulettes.

In 1845, an application, one of many, was made by the colonel of the 74th for the resumption of Highland dress. This was favourably considered and the Adjutant General wrote on 13 August that he would recommend to 'Her Majesty that the Seventy-Fourth regiment should be permitted to resume the appellation of a Highland regiment'. In the *Gazette* of 14 November a War Office memorandum appeared approving the 74th calling itself 'Highland' and allowing the wearing of tartan trews, 'plaid cap' and plaid as worn by the 71st, providing they could keep up their strength with Highland recruits.

On 1 April, the date of the adoption of the Highland clothing, plaid cap and trews by the 74th, a new edition of *Dress Regulations* appeared. The regiment and the 71st were described under the section dealing with Highland regiments and at the end of the section it was added that '*The 71st Highland Light Infantry and the 74th Regiment are each permitted to wear a Tartan plaid scarf, and a special Cap, of regimental pattern. The 71st, 72nd and 74th, wear the trews on all occasions.*'

The 74th adopted the plaid cap, but it differed from that of the 71st in that the officers had a diced band, a white-over-red ball and a star plate. The 74th adopted the black flounders and cap lines for all ranks. The tartan adopted was Lamont which was a lighter blue and green than the 'government' tartan with a white overstripe – white being the facing colour of the regiment. As the 74th was a Highland regiment, the other ranks wore wing epaulettes, as did all officers below the rank of field officer.

The 1846 regulations described the new pattern of shako taken into use by the infantry in 1844. The 71st had 'cocked' their bonnets to the new shape and the 74th adopted this pattern in 1846.

Soon after the adoption of the new pattern, the 71st adopted bronzed fittings to the cap. The 74th cap had gilt fittings and a plate in the shape of the star of the Order of the Thistle with a circle in the centre surmounted by the crown. Around the outer edge of the circle was the word 'Highlanders' and within the number '74'.

The 74th wore the same forage cap as the kilted Highland regiments (see p 55) but the 71st, being light infantry, had a green cloth forage cap with a diced band with the bugle horn and number with above, on the green cloth, a thistle in gold embroidery.

The regiment wearing the bonnet, the 72nd, was dressed and accoutred in the same way as the 74th, except of course for the head-dress. An officer of 1848 is shown in plates 31 and 32, which clearly shows the Highland-pattern coatee, the laced collar and slashed cuff flaps, as well as the epaulettes adorned with a thistle. The bonnet badge, just visible in the lower left of the painting was as fig 12 and appears to have been worn from about 1825 to 1881. As it was for other infantry officers, the frock coat was discontinued in 1848 and the shell jacket worn. It was revived again – this time double-breasted without the shoulder scales – in 1852.

Plate 33 shows a group of officers of the 71st photographed by Roger Fenton in the Crimea. The two officers on the left are wearing the scarlet shell jacket with buff collar and cuffs, the 1852-pattern forage cap with diced band, 'French horn' badge with thistle above and tartan trews. The officer on the extreme left wears a black waist-belt with slings on the left side to support the broadsword in a black leather scabbard with steel mounts. The officer to his right wears the crimson sash and a dirk on the right front. The other officers are wearing sheepskin coats except for the officer on the far right who wears a blue(?) jacket and a forage cap with neither badge nor peak.

PLATE 31 *Officer of the 72nd Highlanders, c 1848. Although termed Highlanders and dressed as such, they wore tartan trews.*

PLATE 32 *Officers and men, 72nd Highlanders, 1854. This plate shows the front and rear view of the uniform worn by non-kilted Highland regiments.*

FIGURE 12 *Glengarry badges:* (top, left to right) *25th Foot; 72nd Foot; 75th Foot.* (bottom, left to right) *93rd Foot; 73rd Foot; 92nd Foot – all c 1874.*

Non-kilted regiments 1855–1881

In 1855, the new double-breasted doublet was introduced for the army and the non-kilted Highland regiments that received them were the 71st, 72nd and 74th, the first and last of which wore a special-pattern cap, while the 72nd wore the bonnet, cocked and feathered.

In the series of photographs of Crimean heroes referred to (p 58) there are two depicting the doublet worn by the 72nd with bonnet and trews and the white doublet worn by a bandsman of the same regiment. Plate 34 shows three privates of the 72nd wearing the double-breasted doublets with diamond-shaped buttons. The men are wearing the 1852 equipment consisting of a waist-belt and single cross-

◁ PLATE 33 *Officers of 71st Highlanders in the Crimea, 1855 (from an original photograph by Roger Fenton).*

belt. They are also wearing the extra black ammunition pouch on the right front and appear only to have a small pocket without flap for the percussion caps, to the right of the fastening of the doublet above the ammunition pouch (see plate 24), where the pocket in the doublet has a flap). The knapsack can be clearly seen with mess tin and regimental number, as well as the connecting strap worn across the chest linking the two shoulder-straps. The private on the right, Harper, is wearing the undress bonnet with a bugle denoting the light company of the regiment. He also wears a good conduct 'badge', introduced in about 1836, on the right lower arm. The regimental facing colour was buff.

Plate 35 shows a drummer of the 72nd wearing the white doublet with diamond-shaped buttons. As the 72nd was a regiment which used buff facings, the collar and cuffs of the white band doublets were red (regiments with white facings also wore red collar and cuffs). The photograph also shows the band lace around the collar and down the seam of the arm as well as on the Inverness skirts and around the slashed flap on the cuff which was peculiar to the regiment. Wing epaulettes were retained for the band. The waist-belt supports a band sword on the right hip – in Scottish Highland regiments, a broad sword. Badges of rank or good conduct 'badges' were in red on the white doublet.

The 71st and 74th would have been dressed in a similar manner but with the shako for each regiment in place of the bonnet. The 71st appears to have had a white pouch fitted to the cross-belt for percussion caps, rather than a pocket in the doublet.

The continuity of the uniform of the various Scottish regiments dressed as ordinary infantry of the line is illustrated by the various major changes in dress, which are listed below under date.

1856   Single-breasted tunic replaced double-breasted one adopted 1855. New shako adopted 16 January 1855 came into general use.
1859   Leather leggings introduced in the infantry to be worn in marching order.
1861   New-pattern shako ordered and authorised on 28 November.
1862   Flank companies and their distinctions abolished.
1866   Regimental-pattern tape used by drummers abolished and a universal pattern of white with red crowns adopted. Officers adopt a blue patrol jacket in place of the frock coat. Fusiliers adopt a fur cap made of sealskin.

1868   Slashed flap on the cuffs abolished and pointed cuffs introduced, edged with gold lace and braid for officers.
1869   New-pattern shako introduced with gold lace for officers and a new pattern of plate. Other ranks' shako ornamented with red and black braid.
1870   All-red ball-tuft introduced for royal regiments.
1871   Other ranks' cuffs ornamented with a trefoil in white tape. Racoon-skin cap introduced for fusiliers. A submission of 2 August recommended that the brick-red cloth of other ranks' tunics be abolished and scarlet used for all ranks.
1873   Shoulder-straps of the tunic changed to scarlet, edged with white tape and numerals ordered to be in white metal instead of embroidered. Regimental-pattern buttons discontinued for other ranks and 'general service' button substituted. White tunics discontinued for band wear. New scarlet 'frock' tunic introduced for training, drill and active service.
1874   The glengarry in plain blue with black silk binding introduced for other ranks in place of the forage cap. Light-infantry hair plume replaced with a ball-tuft.
1878   Spiked helmet in blue cloth introduced by General Order 40 in May to replace the shako. Depot companies continued with the shako until 1881. The helmet had a brass spike and star plate with the regimental number in the centre. Brass chin-chains were fitted to rosettes each side.
1881   Regiments linked and given Territorial titles.

A new edition of *Dress Regulations* appeared, in 1857, which described the single-breasted doublet introduced in that year and the new shako for the infantry – amongst other changes. In the section 'Highland Regiments', referring to the non-kilted 71st, 72nd and 74th, the following appears:

The 71st Highland Light Infantry and the 74th Regiment are each permitted to wear a Tartan plaid scarf, and a special Cap of regimental pattern, deposited at Army Clothing Department.
The 71st, 72nd and 74th wear the trews on all occasions.

A badge for the forage cap was described for the 72nd and 71st, the 74th being ordered to wear the 'number of the regiment in gold embroidery on the band and a gold embroidered thistle above'. The 72nd was to wear on the cap 'a small star upon the thistle' and the 71st to have 'a

PLATE 34 *Privates Noble, Dawson and Harper, 72nd Highlanders, 1856, showing the new double-breasted tunic introduced that year. Private Harper (right) wears the undress bonnet with stringed bugle-horn badge, denoting him as a light-company man.*

PLATE 35 *Drummer John Rennie, 72nd Highlanders, 1856, showing the new-pattern jacket in white for band and with regimental-pattern tape around the collar, cuffs and seams. Notice also the wing epaulettes retained for bands.*

78

gold embroidered horn bugle with a small thistle in centre, above the gold number'. This replaced the earlier badge shown in the Fenton photograph (plate 33).

The new shako was introduced in 1855 but first mentioned in 1857 *Dress Regulations*. The shako measured $5^1/_4$in in front and $7^1/_8$in at the back, sloping forward from the back and coming further down the back of the head. In the 71st, the top and bottom were bound with black thistle-pattern lace with black cord festoon and cap lines, terminating in flounders. In the centre of the top band at the front was a black corded boss with metal spray of thistles on it. Behind the boss was fitted the round ball-tuft. In the middle of the front was a bugle-horn badge with the number '71' in the curl. The rank and file adopted the same shape but with the diced band around the bottom. The red tourrie or tuft which was fitted to the top of other ranks' shakos disappeared with the introduction of the lower pattern after the Crimean War.

The 74th adopted the same shape of shako but with a diced band for officers and other ranks and a gilt metal thistle spray on the boss and the same style of plate as worn on the previous shako. The new-pattern shako had a leather chin-strap in place of the chin-chain worn previously by officers.

In the 71st, staff sergeants, who had worn silver lace since 1768, adopted gold lace in 1856, the same year that sergeants of Highland regiments conformed with the other sergeants of the infantry and wore their sashes across the right shoulder instead of the left.

In India, during the mutiny, the 71st wore the white clothing with cover to the forage cap but on certain occasions appear to have worn the white jackets with tartan trews.

In 1862, a new pattern of shako was adopted by the 71st and 74th, based on that approved for infantry on 28 November 1860 and taken into wear during 1861. The shako was the same shape as the previous pattern but lower being only $4^1/_2$in at the front and 7in at the back. The officers of the 71st abandoned the black thistle-pattern lace and now adopted the diced band. The festoons at the front disappeared and a simple braided interwoven cap line was fitted above the peak, with those at the back being two plain cords. The body lines lost the flounders which were replaced by smaller and simpler acorns. The 74th's officers also adopted the new low-pattern shako with the same badge as previously worn but without the crown over the circle. The rank and file of both the 71st and 74th followed suit and continued to have ones without seams but with dicing in the weave. Officers' shakos had the cloth seamed

and the dicing made up of small squares of material sewn together. The 71st had the badge on the shako and the thistle spray on the boss in silver or white metal in place of bronze worn on the previous pattern.

Although in most ways the 26th were treated, dressed and accoutred as a line regiment, there was a diced band on the forage cap of both officers and men. Deviations from established pattern without authority were always frowned on and discouraged and so, on 15 January 1858, the Deputy Adjutant General, T. Troutbridge, requested the officer commanding the 26th Regimental Depot to state 'whether any written authority exists for any deviation from the established pattern forage cap'. The commanding officer, Colonel A. T. Hemphill, replied from Bermuda, where the regiment was stationed, that 'there is no written authority with the Regiment for any deviation' but he followed this up swiftly with the argument for retaining it: 'the present Bandmaster (a man of the highest respectability) states that the officers and men wore the same pattern Forage Cap as they now do when he joined the "Cameronians" in the year 1827.'

The colonel ended by asking that the diced band be retained. The Horse Guards replied in March that the present pattern should be continued.

In 1863, the 71st was involved in the 'Umbeyla Campaign' and a sketch book of Captain Howard reveals that the men wore red serge single-breasted jackets without facings, trews and a white helmet with red puggaree. The greatcoats with capes, grey for the officers and blue for the men, were carried rolled, bandolier-fashion over the left shoulder.

The previous year, the 75th Foot were allowed to be styled 75th or Stirlingshire but no concessions were made concerning Highland dress. In 1863, however, the 75th Regiment was given permission to have a diced band on the Kilmarnock forage cap. This distinction was continued on the glengarry when it was adopted. In 1865, the 91st was restored to the Highland establishment. The change was notified in a War Office memorandum of 3 May 1864 ordering the 91st to resume the title of Argyllshire Highlanders and ordering the wearing of the Highland jacket, Campbell tartan trews and a similar shako to the 71st and 74th. The white waistcoat, however, worn by other Highland regiments, was denied to them. In 1865, the small white buff pouch worn on the cross-belt to carry percussion caps was removed and a pocket put on the front of the ammunition pouches under the flap.

Plate 36 shows a private and a corporal of the 74th in marching and drill order. The man on the left wears the

PLATE 36 *Private Scott and Corporal Browne, 74th Highlanders, 1866, in the single-breasted doublet. Notice the corporal in white-sleeved waistcoat and with 'pork-pie' forage cap with diced band and number. Private Scott (right) wears the oilskin cover to the shako and gaiters in marching order.*

new-pattern shako with the red doublet with slashed flap on the cuff and Inverness skirts. The white pouch was still worn on the cross-belt and the black ammunition pouch on the front right of the belt had given way to a white one. The knapsack with mess tin in oilskin cover is worn on the back. In heavy marching order and inclement weather, an oilskin cover was provided for the cap and the ball-tuft was not worn. Black leggings were also worn. The corporal in drill order wears the Kilmarnock with diced band and badge above the band. The white jacket has twisted white shoulder-cords and two buttons at the cuff. The corporal's chevrons in red are worn on both arms.

In 1868, a blue patrol jacket of blue cloth, bound around with black mohair braid and ornamented on the chest with frogging and toggles, was introduced for officers. The back seams were also ornamented in braid of black mohair. The sword was worn from a belt under the jacket.

In the same year, the slashed flap was abolished and the gauntlet cuff adopted by Highland regiments which included the 71st, 72nd, 74th and 91st.

In 1870, the Kilmarnock bonnet was discontinued and the glengarry substituted for other ranks. In 1870, the new valise equipment was introduced (see p 63) and Queen Victoria ordered that 'soft tartan' should replace the 'hard tartan' in Highland regiments. Field officers were ordered in this year to have $5/8$in bars of lace at the top of their shakos, according to rank: colonels, three; lt-colonels, two; and majors, one.

On 21 March 1871, 100 picked men of the 91st furnished a guard of honour on the occasion of the marriage of the Princess Louise, to the Marquis of Lorne, as a result of which Queen Victoria commanded that the 91st should always march past in quick time to their pipers and that the regiment should in future be designated the Princess Louise's Argyllshire Highlanders and should bear as its colours the crest and motto of the Argyll family, which was ' Boar's head with *Ne obliviscaris* – with the Princess Louise's coronet and cypher on the three corners of the regimental colour'.

This was authorised by a War Office memorandum of 2 April 1872. This badge was, however, not authorised for the forage cap, shako or officers' buttons.

Pipers were allowed in Highland regiments only at the officers' expense prior to 1854 but at public expense thereafter. Even so, the 91st and 92nd were refused permission to have pipers in 1852. The 26th, a Scottish Lowland regiment, managed to keep pipers – and at public expense – by bearing them on the strength as privates. In June 1862 the commanding officer received a memorandum from the brigade major of the 2nd Brigade at Aldershot asking on what authority were men employed as pipers in the 26th. The commanding officer replied that the bandmaster had told him that in his thirty-five years of service men had been enlisted as pipers but added conveniently that 'no trace of the original authority or date . . . exists.' They had, the colonel continued, been returned as rank and file usually.

However irregular the practice of returning the pipers as rank and file was, or even having them at all, the authorities acquiesced and permission was given to keep the pipers: 'no alteration as to these pipers is required.' In 1865, the 26th requested that a private of the depot of the regiment be employed as a piper and again the request was granted.

In 1870, the red doublets gave way to scarlet ones and in 1873 shoulder-straps were changed to the facing colour and white metal numerals placed on them instead of embroidery, while regimental buttons were replaced for other ranks by a general-service button. At the same time collar badges were taken into wear.

In 1874, a further edition of *Dress Regulations* appeared and the details concerning the 71st, 72nd, 74th and 91st were as for the Highland regiments (see pp 63–64). The regulations, however, stipulated certain special items for the regiments wearing trews, shoulder-plaid and brooch. The shako was described as:

> For the 71st, 74th and 91st Highlanders – blue cloth, of the same shape and dimensions as for Infantry of the Line, with diced band, black cord ornament and plate of special pattern, green tuft in the 71st Light Infantry, red and white in the 74th and 91st.

The forage cap described for the non-kilted regiments (Highland kilted regiments had adopted the glengarry) was described as:

> Dark green cloth in the 71st Light Infantry, blue cloth in the 72nd, 74th and 91st regiments. Diced band with red piping round the crown. The number of the regiment embroidered in gold on the band in front, with a thistle in the centre for the 71st, a thistle with a small star on the thistle for the 72nd and a thistle for the 74th and 91st regiments. Embroidered peak and chin strap.

Officers of the non-kilted regiments were ordered leggings akin to those worn by the men in marching order. Mess dress, the same as worn by kilted regiments, made its appearance at this time, the 71st wearing the old drill

jackets with the collar turned down, showing the cherry-coloured lining but fitting to it the gold shoulder cords of the shell jacket, which had trefoil ends. The waistcoat was white.

The serge doublet was introduced for officers in about 1878 and was similar in appearance to that adopted by the men in 1873. The doublet was single-breasted with the familiar gauntlet-pattern cuffs. The front was cut to slope away and the Inverness skirts were omitted. On the pocket flaps each side below the waist and on the gauntlet cuffs were three strands of gold braid and buttons – those of the rank and file being white worsted – and general-service buttons. The collar only was in the facing colour, the cuffs and shoulder-straps being scarlet. Ranking for officers was removed from the collar on this garment and worn on the shoulder-straps. The system of denoting ranking by additional bands of lace around the cuff was adhered to and narrow bands of braid were placed around the top of the gauntlet cuff.

The 91st was the only Highland regiment to be involved in the Zulu War of 1877–9 and photographs taken at the time reveal the serge doublet in use and many other details of the uniform.

A photograph of a group of officers (in the National Army Museum N/PH 9715) shows them wearing the white helmet with a band of regimental tartan around it, as introduced in the 1870s. Officers are wearing trews and knee boots and with their swords hanging (they have the active-service cross hilt and not the basket guard) from white waist-belts, only a single officer wearing what appears to be a Sam Browne belt. Revolvers, binoculars and so on were carried in brown leather holsters and pouches by various and often numerous brown leather straps worn across the body. One officer in the photograph is wearing the full-dress doublet with gauntlet cuffs in the facing colour and twisted gold shoulder-cords.

Another photograph of the same regiment shows the men and pipers drawn up ready to march off. In front are the pioneers and behind them the pipers in kilts. The regiment behind is wearing greatcoats bandolier-fashion with black pouches (with the exception of one man in the front row who has buff) to their valise equipment. All are wearing the serge doublet with trews, white helmet and leggings.

In 1880, the 71st was asked by a letter from the Horse Guards dated 23 April to 'furnish me with a copy of the authority for officers of the Regiment under your command wearing cap lines around the neck'.

Although the 71st, 74th and 91st wore the shako with

black cord decoration above the peak and round the back, the last two terminated theirs on the right side, with small acorns hanging down as was done by other ranks of all three regiments. The officers of the 71st, however, attached 'body' lines to the right side of the shako, wore them around the neck and hooked up on the right side of the doublet.

The colonel's reply was that, as far as was known in the regiment, they had worn them ever since being light infantry and certainly did so when he joined in 1830. The 71st, or any other infantry regiment, did not adopt lines until the shako introduced in 1816. In May approval was given to continue using the body lines.

In 1880, the shoulder-plaid, which had been worn by officers, sergeant-major, bugle major (of the 71st) bands and pipers, was ordered to be worn by colour sergeants and sergeants.

The reform that affected the entire infantry came into force in 1881. The first proposals are detailed on p 66, with the addition of the 26th and 74th being combined as the Cameronian Highlanders. However, General Order 41 of 1 May combined the 26th and 90th as the Scotch Rifles (Cameronians) and the 71st and 74th as the Highland Light Infantry. The 26th and 90th were restyled, by General Order 70 of 1 July, the Cameronians (Scotch Rifles). In November of the same year, they became the Cameronians (Scottish Rifles).

Chapter 4 Infantry
1881-1914

Highland regiments   1881-1914

The upheaval caused by the implementation of the Cardwell army reforms, in the linking of previously numbered Highland regiments into two-battalion regiments (the 79th, the Cameron Highlanders, remained a single-battalion regiment) and designating them by a title, brought a number of changes in the uniforms, badges and buttons of the regiments. Perhaps the most important change was the loss of regimental individuality when officers' regimental-pattern lace was abolished and regimental facings were confined to three basic colours and blue for royal regiments. Scottish regiments, except in the case of royal regiments, were to wear yellow facings to the doublet and to have gold lace with thistle pattern. The Gordon Highlanders managed, however, to keep the black line from their previous pattern of lace and this was 'introduced at top and bottom'.

In 1880, prior to the reforms, officers' badges of rank had been removed from the collar and placed on twisted gold shoulder-cords. The *Dress Regulations* of 1883 were the first issued after the linking of regiments with territorial titles and give details of the new facings, badges and buttons. The new regulations repeated exactly the same description of the doublet as that of 1874 but added 'Shoulder-straps of twisted round gold cord, universal pattern, lined with scarlet; a small button of regimental pattern at the top. Badges of rank in silver'.

When the regiments were combined, the problem of sorting out exactly what tartan should be worn arose. Eventually the following was decided: the Royal Highlanders (Black Watch) – as at present (this was the government tartan); the Seaforth Highlanders – Mackenzie; the Gordon Highlanders – Gordon; the Queen's Own Cameron Highlanders – as at present (this was the 79th or Erracht tartan); and the Sutherland and Argyll Highlanders (Princess Louise's) – as at present worn by the 93rd (which was the Sutherland tartan). The rest of the uniform, including the many varied regimental patterns, remained as before but, in place of the previous numbers, new badges were placed on the belt-plates, dirk scabbards, cross-belt plates (fig 13), brooches and sword blades. The regulations, however, do not mention any specific types of head-dress, only that the matter was 'not yet decided'. The authorities could not make up their minds exactly what type of head-dress would be suitable and were considering putting Highlanders – as they had done Lowland regiments and the Scottish Rifles – into the infantry cloth-covered helmet. The Highland Light Infantry (the 71st and 74th combined) were, however, permitted to continue to use the special pattern of shako and wore the same uniform as before with yellow facings to their doublets (plate 37).

The badges decided upon for the Highland regiments

PLATE 37 *Officer, private and bugler of the Highland Light Infantry (71st and 74th), 1882 (from an original watercolour by R. Simkin).*

and the design of button for officers (other ranks continued with the general service button introduced in 1876) are taken from *Dress Regulations*, 1883:

The Black Watch (Royal Highlanders): badge (fig 13). Button – within the designation 'The Royal Highlanders, Black Watch', the Star of the Order of the Thistle, recessed; on the centre of the star, a circle; within the circle, St Andrew and cross. Collar badge – St Andrew and cross in silver. Belt-plate – on a *seeded* rectangular plate with burnished edges, badge as for bonnet but smaller.

Officers of the regiment were allowed to wear the old-pattern badges and buttons after 1881 until replacements were needed, although all new officers had to provide themselves with the new patterns on joining. The glengarry badge with '42' in the centre was sometimes worn by officers and sergeants of the 1st Battalion until the mid-1920s.

The Highland Light Infantry: badge (fig 13). Button – Star of the Order of the Thistle; on the star, a horn; in the centre of the horn, the monogram 'H.L.I.'; above the horn, the crown as represented in the collar of the Order of the Star of India; below the horn a scroll, inscribed 'Assaye'; under the scroll, the elephant. Collar-badge – same as the head-dress badge in white metal for other ranks but in silver with H.L.I.), scroll with 'Assaye' and elephant in gilt metal. Belt-plate – special pattern; frosted gilt rectangular plate with badge as for 'Chaco'.

Seaforth Highlanders (Ross-shire Buffs, the Duke of Albany's): badge (fig 13) – other ranks did not have the coronet and cypher of the Duke of Albany, a letter 'L' above the stag's head. Button – a stag's head with the cypher of HRH, the Duke of Albany above, a scroll beneath inscribed 'Seaforth Highlanders'. Collar-badge – two badges were worn with the cypher of HRH, the late Duke of York with scroll, inscribed 'Caber Feidh' and the elephant. Belt-plate – special pattern; rectangular plate entirely gilt, burnished with the same badge as the head-dress but smaller and with motto on the scroll 'Tulloch Ard'.

The Gordon Highlanders: badge (fig 13). Button – the cross of St Andrew; on the cross a thistle wreath joined to a scroll let into the upper divisions of the cross and inscribed 'Gordon Highlanders'; within the scroll, on the upper divisions of the cross, the sphinx over Egypt; within

the wreath on the lower divisions of the cross, the Royal Tiger over India. Collar badge – the Royal Tiger; in gold embroidery for the officers, in metal for the rank and file. Belt-plate – burnished gilt rectangular plate, with, in silver, the badge as on the buttons, but larger.

The Queen's Own Cameron Highlanders: badge (fig 13). Button – within the designation 'The Queen's Own Cameron Highlanders' the thistle surmounted by the crown. Collar badge – the thistle surmounted by the crown; in silver embroidery for the officers but in metal for the rank and file. Belt-plate – burnished gilt rectangular plate; in silver on the plate, a thistle wreath; within the wreath, St Andrew with cross.

Princess Louise's (Argyll and Sutherland Highlanders): badge (fig 43). Button – a myrtle wreath interlaced with a wreath of butcher's broom; within the myrtle wreath, a boar's head on a scroll inscribed 'Ne obliviscaris'; within the wreath of butcher's broom, a cat on scroll inscribed 'Sans peur'; a label of three points above the boar's head and the cat; above the wreaths, the coronet of HRH, the Princess Louise. Collar-badge – the same as the button but without the coronet of Princess Louise above the wreaths. Belt-plate – burnished gilt rectangular plate with the same design as for the collar in silver fitted to it; above the wreaths, in frosted silver, a scroll surmounted by the coronet of the Princess; the scroll inscribed 'Princess Louise's'; below the wreath a silver scroll inscribed 'Argyll and Sutherland Highlanders'.

The regulations of 1883 described the shell jacket as being of scarlet cloth and add that the 'Gordon Highlanders' had 'double narrow braid, with a black centre'. The forage cap for wear with trews was authorised only for the Seaforths and Gordons but the glengarry was ordered for all, except the Highland Light Infantry, whose other ranks, but not the officers, wore the glengarry. The

FIGURE 13 *Cap badges, c 1904:* (top, left to right) ▷ *Royal Scots Greys; Seaforth Highlanders (72nd and 78th); Royal Scots (1st).* (Second row) *Scottish Rifles (26th and 90th); Royal Scots Fusiliers (21st); King's Own Scottish Borderers (25th).* (Third row) *Gordon Highlanders (75th and 92nd); Black Watch (42nd and 73rd); Highland Light Infantry (71st and 74th).* (Fourth row) *Argyll and Sutherland Highlanders (91st and 93rd); Queen's Own Cameron Highlanders (79th).*

glengarry was ordered to be plain in the Royal Highlanders, Seaforths and Camerons, diced in the Gordons and Argyll and Sutherlands. In the Highland Light Infantry, the glengarry was plain for the men. The forage cap for the officers was similar in shape to that of other infantry officers but in green cloth with a diced band. Officers under field rank had a crimson cloth welt on their caps.

There were a great many changes in regimental uniforms during the early 1880s which mainly affected the other ranks. In the Black Watch, the formation of a two-battalion regiment under one title on amalgamation with the 73rd brought about the disappearance of Royal Stewart tartan. Pipers of the 42nd had worn this tartan back in the eighteenth century but had at some date reverted to the government tartan until 1840, when the Royal Stewart was restored. Between then and 1860, it once more disappeared but Queen Victoria gave her approval for its restoration in September 1889 and in April 1890 it was once more taken into wear.

In 1883 the badges of rank for officers were changed. In place of the two symbols – the crown, and the star worn alone with lace and braid to show rank – the new method was to group stars and crown together to give each officer an individual and easily recognisable rank without having to resort to studying the braiding. From 'General Instructions' of *Dress Regulations 1883*, the ranking is given as:

Colonel – Crown and two stars below.

Lieutenant-Colonel – Crown and one star below.

Major – Crown.

Captain – Two stars.

Lieutenant – One star.

Second Lieutenant – No badge.

Even though the announcement of the new regiments had taken place in 1881, it was not until the following year that the new-pattern dress was distributed. The 91st, for example, who linked with the 93rd, did not receive the kilt until May 1882.

In 1882, two Highland regiments, with the Highland Light Infantry, embarked for Egypt to take part in the campaign under Sir Garnet Wolseley. Both the 1st Battalion, Black Watch, and the Queen's Own Cameron Highlanders wore frock doublets, white helmets and the kilt. Plate 38, a watercolour by R. Simkin of 1882, shows the Queen's Own in the service dress worn in Egypt. The Black Watch uniform was the same design, except of course for the red hackle worn in the folds of the puggaree on the left of the helmet. The 2nd Battalion, Highland Light Infantry, was still wearing trews in the old Lamont

tartan when it fought in Egypt wearing the frock doublet and white helmet.

In 1882, an 'improved' valise equipment was authorised, which had newly designed pouches which were larger and flatter and the valise was replaced by a square 'boxed' knapsack similar to that worn with the old cross-belt equipment. It was entirely in black oilskin cloth with reinforced leather corners and had the regimental title, in a shortened form, painted in white in the centre. The 1882 equipment can be seen in plate 28, with the new pouches, while the old pattern is shown in plate 38, with the smaller fatter pouches. It is very doubtful if the new equipment was issued in time for the 1882 campaign and no contemporary paintings show it in use.

The main alteration in the dress of the other ranks was the change of the facing colour to yellow or blue, depending on regiment, the new collar badges and bonnet badges, which were also worn on the sporran, and the change from white metal numerals on the scarlet shoulder-straps to white embroidered ones with a shortened version of the regimental title. These were 'R.H.' for the Black Watch; 'H.L.I.' and bugle horn, for the Highland Light Infantry; 'SEAFORTH' for the Seaforth Highlanders; 'GORDON' for the Gordon Highlanders; 'CAMERON' for the Cameron Highlanders and 'A. & S.H.' for the Argyll and Sutherland Highlanders.

In the Highland Light Infantry, the brooch was taken back into wear for officers in 1886 and the sash worn with the plaid. In the 2nd Battalion, Black Watch, sergeants wore a blue patrol jacket, with broad braid around the front and on the pocket openings. This fastened by hooks and eyes and was entirely unofficial, being permitted for off-duty in barracks only and at the personal expense of the sergeants concerned. In 1884, on the second Egyptian expedition, the red frock doublets were replaced by ones in light grey and photographs of officers of the Black Watch in about 1886 show that the garment was cut like a patrol jacket with a square front, although some officers had had the ends rounded to clear the sporran. When greatcoats were worn (which were grey for the infantry at this period), valise and belts were worn over the top but 'sergeants will not wear the sash outside the great-coat'. If

PLATE 38 *Officer and private, Queen's Own Cameron Highlanders (79th), dressed for active service in Egypt, 1882 (from an original watercolour by R. Simkin). Note the improved equipment and the 'frock' doublet, without Inverness skirts, being worn.*

the Guard was cloaked, the hackle case was worn but if not, when the Guard marched off, the case was removed. Between retreat and reveille, trews and forage cap were worn. In summer (16 March to 15 November) white jackets were worn with the forage cap but on Sundays the scarlet doublet was worn. In winter the doublet was worn but the plaid was reserved for Sunday, except by the band and pipers who wore it at all times.

Spats were always worn in conjunction with trews by other ranks, except 'by clerks in different offices and school assistants'. In 1886, officers were ordered to wear dirks in review order, except for mounted officers. In the following year a letter from Horse Guards directed that medals, which hitherto had been worn in rather a haphazard fashion, should be worn in line with the top button of the doublet – but most contemporary photographs show the medals worn in line with the second button.

A new pattern of equipment was introduced in 1888 for the army – that designed by Colonel Slade and Lt-Colonel Wallace and called the Slade-Wallace equipment. Although made of the same material as the previous equipment, white buff leather, it departed from the old design in having a waist-belt with braces that fitted to the front, passed over the shoulders, crossed and fitted back to the waist-belt behind. The pouches, again of a new pattern to use with the new ·303 Lee-Metford rifle, were fitted each side at the front and a valise was reintroduced. It was worn high on the shoulders and held by straps that passed through brass 'D's on the cross-braces and buckled to the braces at the front, just above the pouches. Beneath the valise was carried the 'D'-shaped mess tin, in use since about 1816 and on the waist-belt was rolled the greatcoat, blanket or cloak. The equipment is shown in plate 39, a photograph of a corporal of the Black Watch in 1899. The haversack was still carried across the body as was the waterbottle, which changed from the 'Italian' pattern – a barrel-shaped canteen in wood made by Guglielminitti Brothers of Milan – to an enamelled-metal one covered in felt. With the equipment, an entrenching tool was issued which was fitted to the belt alongside the bayonet frog.

In 1891, a new pattern of drill and mess-dress jacket was adopted by Highland regiments, distinct from that which had been previously ordered 'as for Line'. It was first described in the *Dress Regulations* of 1894.

PLATE 39 *Corporal, Black Watch (42nd and 73rd), in khaki foreign-service dress, 1899. Notice the red hackle worn in the puggaree of the sun helmet.*

The Highland bonnet, which had always been described as 'Feather bonnets of authorised pattern', differed from one regiment to another. In the first place the dicing was red, white and blue for royal regiments, the Black Watch and the Queen's Own Cameron Highlanders and red, white and green for others, except the Argyll and Sutherland Highlanders who had only red and white. The Black Watch also had four tails, the Seaforths, Gordons and Camerons five tails and the Argyll and Sutherlands six tails. Hackles were all white except in the case of the Black Watch who wore all red.

The drill and mess jacket is described in the regulations of 1894 for the first time. Each regiment was distinguished by the facing colour and also the lining. In the Black Watch the jacket had buff silk lining – except for the collar which was dark blue – and 'no facing cloth on the inside', while the Argyll and Sutherlands had pale-yellow lining and facing cloth inside the collar and down the inside each side. The Seaforths had buff silk lining with buff cloth on the 'inside of jacket in front and inside of collar', while the Camerons had 'buff silk lining, and no facing cloth on the inside'. The Gordon Highlanders had the jacket lined with red and the collar and inside lined with crimson silk. The mess waistcoat was either in the facing colour, scarlet or tartan, the Gordons being ordered scarlet with a roll collar and three buttons. Plate 40 shows an officer of the Queen's Own Cameron Highlanders in mess dress while plate 41 shows the jacket as worn in drill order. The Highland Light Infantry, however, continued to wear the mess jacket as for infantry of the line.

PLATE 40 *Officer, Queen's Own Cameron Highlanders (79th), in mess dress, 1890 (from an original watercolour by R. Simkin).*

PLATE 41 *Officer, Queen's Own Cameron Highlanders (79th), in drill order, c 1890 (from an original watercolour by R. Simkin).*

The forage cap worn with trews by officers was authorised only for the Seaforths and Gordons and was in blue with a diced band. The officer in plate 28 is wearing this cap. Other officers of the rest of the Highland regiments wore the glengarry as previously, the same pattern as the men. In the Highland Light Infantry, the forage cap was also worn by the officers but in green cloth with a diced band, while for 'Active Service and Peace Manoeuvres' a new pattern of side cap, similar to that worn by the infantry, was ordered but in green cloth. This was the 'Austrian' pattern of cap, which had flaps that turned down to cover the ears. In the regiment, however, this pattern was ignored and the officers continued to wear a green glengarry with diced band and the men a plain green one.

In 1895–6, as a result of the change in rifle drill when the 'long shoulder' was abolished in preference to the 'slope', red and white shoulder pads were issued to protect the doublet or red serge summer doublet and the white drill jacket from oil when holding the rifle at the slope. These pads slipped over the shoulder-strap and buttoned to the first two buttons of the doublet. However, in 1896 there was a more far-reaching change in the dress of the army and the Highland regiments. In that year foreign-service khaki service dress was introduced, but full dress was still retained for home wear (plate 42). In the Highland regiments it was worn with the kilt and hose and spats but in the Highland Light Infantry with trews and khaki puttees. Men in Highland regiments who constituted the 'Regimental Transport' had for some time been wearing Bedford-cord breeches and blue puttees with the red serge tunic, and they continued to wear breeches with the khaki jacket.

The use of khaki or camouflaged clothing was, however, not new. Various attempts had been made since the 1840s to provide a more suitable clothing for fighting than red or scarlet. In 1835, the 71st, amongst other regiments, was ordered to Canada and the men were to be 'Clothed in grey – a cloth very much the colour of the bark of a tree'. During the Kaffir War of 1851–2, the 74th wore trousers, forage cap and Holland bush shirts. During the Indian Mutiny various khaki uniforms were worn (see Chapter 3, pp 59–61) and the 93rd were recorded as wearing 'very ugly brown coats of Stout cotton material with red collar and cuffs, intended for boat work in China'. After the Indian Mutiny a khaki-drill summer dress was adopted in India and on 21 May 1858 the Adjutant General issued the following order:

With the concurrence of the Government, the com-

mander-in-chief is pleased to direct that white clothing shall be discontinued in the European regiments of the Honourable Company's army; and that for the future the summer-clothing of the European soldiers shall consist of two suits of 'khakee', corresponding in pattern and material with the clothing recently sanctioned for the Royal Army of England.

Old white summer clothing was permitted to be worn out but on renewal 'khakee' was to be adopted. The order went on to state 'Commanding Officers will take steps to obtain patterns from regiments of Her Majesty's service. A complete suit including cap cover, should not exceed in cost four-twelve rupees.'

In 1864, however, khaki was abolished as working dress in India, being considered unsmart and on the whole no better dress than that of the sweepers.

During the Afghan War of 1878–9, dyed khaki-drill clothing and white helmets were issued and by the early 1880s khaki service dress was well established in India. During the Ashanti War of 1874, British officers had worn khaki Norfolk jackets and trousers, as well as cork helmets with puggarees – even the commander-in-chief, Sir Garnet Wolseley, adopting this dress. In 1884, khaki field-service dress, consisting of helmet, tunic, trousers and puttees were authorised for all troops in India, Highland regiments wearing the kilt, hose and khaki spats and the Highland Light Infantry, trews.

At last the British government acquiesced in 1896 and ordered a khaki foreign-service dress for each soldier of the British Army proceeding overseas. In *Dress Regulations* of 1894 'hot' climate clothing for officers was only prescribed for Bermuda, China, Straits Settlements, Ceylon, Cyprus, Mauritius, West Indies and Malta (off-parade at the last-named station and at the option of the wearer); but this referred only to white clothing. Khaki 'may be worn under local regulations at . . . Egypt, Straits Settlements, West Coast of Africa'.

It was the Boer War that firmly established the use of khaki, although it had been the issue clothing in the Sudan campaign of 1898. Highland regiments still continued to wear the kilt with sporran and the Highland Light Infantry wore their trews with khaki puttees.

In 1888, there had been established in the British Army an organisation of mounted-infantry troops to provide a

PLATE 42 *Field officer and regimental sergeant-major, Argyll ▷ and Sutherland Highlanders (91st and 93rd), 1896.*

mobile trained force for all emergencies in open country such as found in South Africa. In 1896, mounted infantry were sent to the Cape of Good Hope and a Highland mounted-infantry company was included.

The regiments selected to form this Highland company were 1st Battalion, Seaforth Highlanders, 2nd Battalion, Royal Highlanders (Black Watch), 2nd Battalion, Gordon Highlanders and the 2nd Battalion, the Argyll and Sutherland Highlanders. The uniform of the Highland mounted infantry is illustrated by plate 43, which shows Sergeant Seymour of the 2nd Gordon Highlanders. He is wearing the glengarry with the white undress shell jacket with ranking chevrons in red tape and Bedford-cord breeches and blue puttees. He wears the white Slade-Wallace pattern of waist-belt, which holds the bayonet in a frog on the left side and a brown leather bandolier with loops for single rounds. Note the leather 'bucket' in which the butt of the rifle was placed and carried upright with the sling around the arm to the rear of the saddle. Later this bucket was worn higher to stop the rider using the rifle as a rest, because this resulted in giving the horse a sore back.

PLATE 43   *Sergeant of Highland Mounted Infantry, 1896.*

Plate 39 shows a corporal of the Black Watch in the dress worn in the Sudan. The tunic is the ordinary pattern worn by the rest of the infantry, with unwhitened equipment and white helmet with khaki cover and the red hackle in the left side. The uniform worn was exactly the same as that worn the following year on the outbreak of the South African War. The Black Watch moved directly from India to South Africa and arrived wearing the same uniform that was worn by all troops (except of course for the kilt) in India and the Mediterranean. In 1900, khaki aprons which covered the front of the kilt only and had a pocket to replace the sporran were issued for kilted regiments. Officers wore a similar uniform but with the Sam Browne belt, braces and sword frog, while mounted officers wore pantaloons and dark puttees or riding boots.

The Highland Light Infantry embarked for South Africa wearing khaki but with trews in the regimental tartan and khaki puttees; but not long after their arrival, khaki trousers were issued. The regiment, along with other Highland regiments, wore a square patch of tartan on the left side of the helmets with the officers having an extra triangular patch at the back to distinguish them. Regiments of the line used the old shoulder-straps of the frock tunics which bore the regimental name or initials in white embroidery and sewed these to the helmets. Until May 1900, all troops going to South Africa took a suit of khaki drill and one of khaki serge but after that date two serge suits were supplied. Troops arriving from India were dressed in drill, which was soon exchanged for serge. In May 1900, khaki slouch-hats were issued and the Highland Light Infantry decorated these with cock feathers on the turned-up left side but in September of the same year helmets were once more issued. Officers found that it was preferable to be dressed like the men to avoid the attention of the Boer marksmen, to whom an officer was a valued target and they adopted the Slade-Wallace equipment, left the badges of rank uncleaned and usually dispensed with swords.

The British khaki uniform had been altered slightly by adding three pleats on the sleeve above the cuff and having a stand and fall collar, fastened with hooks and eyes in conformity to the Indian pattern. In 1900, the last *Dress Regulations* of Queen Victoria's long reign were issued. They illustrated and described the new khaki foreign-service dress, which now had a special jacket for Highland regiments.

The jacket was made of drill or serge with patch pockets, with flaps for Scottish regiments pointed at the ends and hollow in the middle. The cuffs were gauntlet-shaped and the front was rounded to clear the sporran. Officers bore on the shoulder-straps the badge of rank and the regimental designation as worn by the men. These are as described on p 89.

Puttees were to be khaki woollen material which were worn by the Highland Light Infantry. There was no mention of the khaki kilt apron or even the fact that spats and hose were worn with the kilt. A spine protector, regulations stated, 'may be worn when the severity of the climate necessitates it'. Mounted officers were allowed to wear boots or puttees, as long as all were dressed the same.

There were, however, many more orders of dress and also some changes in the new regulations. The doublet and full-dress head-dress, kilt, hose and spats, sporran and plaid were worn in full dress, while the frock and drill jacket were reserved for other occasions – fatigues and so on. In India, and in other hot climates, full-dress head-dress was not worn from the early 1890s, the white helmet sufficing for all uses, with brass spike and chin scales for full dress or with a white-covered zinc button on the top and leather chin-strap for other orders. Red serge clothing was in use for 'Review Order' in cold weather, replaced by white cotton drill for hot weather. All other parades all the year round were conducted in khaki drill.

The *Dress Regulations* of 1900 are interesting in that they are the first 'illustrated' ones issued and, as far as Highland regiments are concerned, described the full-dress and undress sporrans for the first time. The alterations in the existing dress were that the cuffs of the doublet should now be only $3^1/_2$in at the front in place of the previous 4in and that the Inverness skirts were made '8, $7^1/_2$ and 7 inches deep, with skirt-flaps on the first two, $^1/_2$ inch shorter'. Certain of the pre-1881 facings were returned, the Seaforth Highlanders being allowed buff as were the Highland Light Infantry. The brooch was still described as of regimental pattern but not to exceed $3^7/_8$in.

The sporrans are described as 'In the Royal High-landers – White horse-hair. The sporran top is in frosted gilt metal, edged with thistles. Thistle leaves at each side and in the centre. Above the centre thistle St. Andrew and cross. Five gold bullion tassels suspended by looped gold cord.'

The bullion tassels on dress sporrans were not allowed to exceed six in number and had to be removable 'in regiments that do not adopt the undress sporran'. In the Royal Highlanders, the undress sporran was white horse-hair with full-dress top and five black horsehair tassels in patent-leather sockets. There were variations for other regiments:

In the Seaforth Highlanders – White horse-hair. The sporran top is in burnished gilt metal engraved with a thistle on each side. In the centre in silver, two sprays of thistle with scroll inscribed 'Cuidich'n Righ' on the lower bend. On the top of the sprays the scrolls inscribed with some of the honours of the Regiment. Between the sprays a stag's head. Above the stag's head two other scrolls inscribed with the remaining honours of the Regiment. Two long black horse-hair tassels with gilt sockets. Sockets engraved with thistles and leaves.

This sporran was also worn by the regiment in undress.

In the Gordon Highlanders – White horse-hair. Gilt metal top engraved with thistles and ornamental edges. In the centre, badges as for waistplate in silver (see page 86). Five gold pull-on tassels hanging from gold cord. The heads of the tassels in dead and bright gold.

In undress, the regiment wore the same pattern of top and horsehair but with two long black horsehair tassels in gilt engraved sockets, suspended by chains.

In the Cameron Highlanders – Grey horse-hair. Sporran top in frosted gilt metal. In the centre, an elliptical ring, inscribed 'The Queen's Own Cameron Highlanders' within an oak-leaf wreath. Within the ring, on a burnished gilt ground, a thistle surmounted by a crown in silver. On either side of the oak-leaf scroll are sprays of thistles. On the lower portion of the wreath and sprays, a scroll inscribed 'Peninsula, Egypt, Waterloo'. Six gold bullion tassels suspended by blue and gold twisted cords.

In undress, the regiment wore a black horsehair sporran with black leather top with St Andrew and cross between two sprays of thistle in silver. The tassels were two long white horsehair ones in black leather sockets.

In the Argyll and Sutherland Highlanders – Engraved gilt top, special shape (five-sided), square edges with centre in enamel. On the centre, the boar's head and scroll, the coronet with cypher, and the cat and scroll similar in design to the full dress head-dress. Five small gold bullion tassels with netted head suspended by looped gold cords.

In undress, the Argyll and Sutherland wore a sporran with a badger's head forming the top, with six short white horsehair tassels with thistle sockets suspended by looped gold-wire cord.

The *Regulations* noted for the first time that the Highland Light Infantry wore 'Chaco lines' in black silk cord 'with egg mould and sliders' although, of course, they had been wearing them for very many years (see p 83), but did introduce a special pattern of drill and mess jacket which was in scarlet cloth with collar and cuffs in buff. It had gauntlet-pattern cuffs edged in white – as was the collar – with ten buttons down the front and four on the back of each cuff. The shoulder-cords were described as 'Twisted treble gold . . . lined with scarlet', with a silver embroidered thistle below the rank badges. The waistcoat was in authorised regimental tartan with the pockets on each side edged in gold cord forming 'crows feet in the centre and at the ends'.

In undress, officers wore a scarlet frock of 'Red Angola or serge' with collar in the face colour and gauntlet cuffs with five buttons down the front, same colour shoulder-straps and breast pocket. Although this frock is first mentioned in this edition of *Dress Regulations,* it had been adopted in 1898. The mess jacket for the Highland Light Infantry, although again marked as a new item in regulations, had been adopted in 1895.

In 1902, as a result of the South African War, there was a radical change in the uniforms of the army. Many garments were done away with and orders of dress changed and modified. Foreign-service dress remained the same but the innovation was the introduction of a home-service dress. It was introduced by Army Order 10 of 1902 for rank and file and Army Order 40 of the same year for officers.

As the pattern of jacket was common to both Highland and Lowland regiments, it is dealt with in a separate chapter (see Chapter 5, p 105). In 1903 and again in 1908 new patterns of equipment were issued to the infantry for wear with service dress and these two, being common to both Highland and Lowland regiments, are dealt with in Chapter 5.

The various alterations in dress and orders of dress brought about by the introduction of service dress were embodied in a new edition of *Dress Regulations* which appeared in 1904. The various items worn in full dress and review order remained the same, except that there was a change in certain of the regimental-pattern sporrans. The

PLATE 44 *Private, Black Watch (42nd and 73rd), in* ▷
review order, 1910.

Royal Highlanders – the Black Watch – replaced the five bullion tassels and wore the sporran previously reserved for undress. The Argyll and Sutherland Highlanders used the undress sporran with badger's head for all occasions, except levee dress when the previous pattern with gilt top was worn. The Black Watch used the gold bullion tassels on the above-mentioned sporran for levee dress.

The main alteration in the doublet was the abolition of the various lacing and braiding on collar and cuff to distinguish each rank and a new system of lacing was adopted, common to all ranks. There was now only lace around the top of the collar and down the front and around the top of the gauntlet cuff. Braiding was confined to along the bottom of the collar and the button-loops on the cuffs and Inverness skirts. The ranking of junior officers was altered by Army Order 107 of May 1902 which now instructed a captain to have three stars, a lieutenant, two and a second-lieutenant, one. Beside the full dress mentioned above, the other order of dress was undress, which for Highland regiments was regulated as a white jacket worn with the glengarry. The white jacket was to be 'Plain white cloth, stand-up collar, no cuffs, gilt buttons, shoulder cords interchangeable with those of the doublet except Highland Light Infantry, who wear shoulder cords as for mess jacket'. The shoulder-cords were those mentioned on p 84.

The various other orders of dress for India previously mentioned were still worn, except that now for the rank and file the Slade-Wallace equipment was abolished and only the belt, bayonet frog and one pouch worn for review order (plate 44). The main difference was that the pointed white helmet, worn before and during the South African War, had been replaced with the wider-brimmed Wolseley helmet. In place of the 'Star plates' that had been on the foreign-service helmet until just before the turn of the century, puggaree badges, similar to those worn on the glengarry, were worn with the proviso that they were to be fitted 'so . . . as not to perforate either the puggaree or helmet'.

In 1913, the shoulder-straps of other ranks' doublets were ordered to be in the face colour rather than scarlet and, in the Highland Light Infantry, officers and staff sergeants gave up the diced band on the glengarry and adopted an all-green one, as worn by the men.

On the outbreak of war in 1914, full dress was handed into store and its wearing placed in abeyance. In 1919, Army Council Instructions 70 informed officers that they did not need to replace any worn-out items of full dress and were to replace or provide themselves only with service dress until further orders. For the rank and file, full dress never reappeared although it was worn by bands on certain occasions.

Regimental staff of Highland regiments were described in *Dress Regulations* of 1822 as differing only from regimental officers in having a single-breasted jacket, a black feather for 'the Surgeon and his Assistant', not wearing the sash and the sword-belt under the coat. The regulations of 1831 added that the plaid and kilt were not required to be worn but that with the exception of the adjutant, the staff-officers were to wear the same uniform as other officers.

After the Crimea, regimental staff officers are recorded as having a cocked hat, the paymaster with no plume, the quartermaster to have a 5in cock's feather 'mushroom shaped', white and red for line but all white for Highland regiments – except the 42nd who wore all red. The Highland Light Infantry had all green. The surgeon and his assistant wore a blackcock's tail 'drooping from a feathered stem five inches deep' and also wore a black shoulder-belt and a pouch with gilt ornaments, which contained instruments.

The 1874 *Regulations* mentioned that the adjutant and musketry instructor should wear the uniforms of their rank but that the paymaster and quartermaster should wear the uniforms of their rank but with a black morocco waist-belt. The 1883 *Regulations* repeat this but add a black leather cross-belt and pouch and note that the sash, shoulder plaid and brooch were not worn.

In 1904, the black belt worn by the quartermaster disappeared and he assumed the uniform of his rank. Regimental surgeons had disappeared in 1873, when they were grouped into the Medical Staff Corps.

Lowland regiments 1881-1914

Although the upheaval caused by the Cardwell reforms had been a major one for the Highland and kilted regiments, they were even more far reaching and varied for the Lowlands regiments or, as they were referred to in the dress regulations, 'Scottish Regiments (wearing trews)'. The main innovation was that all Scottish regiments now adopted the doublet for officers and all ranks, every regiment – there were three – adopting blue facings and gold thistle-pattern lace for the officers. The tartan decided upon was the government pattern for all regiments. In May 1881, when General Order 41 appeared, the 1st Foot were designated the Lothian Regiment (Royal Scots), the 21st, the Royal Scots Fusiliers but in

PLATE 45 *Drum-major, private, regimental sergeant-major, piper and colour sergeant of the Royal Scots Fusiliers (21st), 1896.*

July, when General Order 70 appeared, the names had been changed to the Royal Scots (Lothian Regiment) and the 25th, in the earlier order given the title of the York Regiment (King's Own Borderers), was redesignated the King's Own Borderers.

The first regulations to cover the uniforms of the new Lowlands regiments were those of 1883. The doublet of the Highland regiments was adopted and worn with trews and the blue cloth helmet which had been used since 1878 by the infantry. A diced band was worn on the forage cap for active service. The Royal Scots Fusiliers were dressed in similar fashion but with a black racoon-skin cap, 9in in height with a gilt grenade on the front with the royal arms on the ball. The fusilier cap with brass grenade was worn by the rank and file.

The various badges ordered for the Lowland regiments were: Royal Scots (Lothian Regiment): badge (fig 13). Button – badge of the Order of the Thistle; below the badge 'The Royal Scots'. Collar-badge – the thistle in gold embroidery on a blue ground. (Other ranks wore the thistle in white metal.) Belt-plate – on a gilt rectangular plate, the star of the Order of the Thistle with circle

inscribed 'Nemo me impune lacessit'; within the circle on a green enamel ground, a thistle in gilt. The King's Own Borderers: badge (fig 13). Button – the royal crest within the designation 'The King's Own Borderers'. Collar-badge – the castle of Edinburgh in silver embroidery on a ground of gold embroidery, battlements etc., picked out in blue silk. (Other ranks wore a metal castle badge.) Belt-plate – the royal crest in silver on a frosted gilt centre; on the circle 'The King's Own Borderers'. Royal Scots Fusiliers: badge (fig 13). Button – the thistle surmounted by the crown. Collar-badge – a grenade in silver embroidery; on the ball of the grenade, the thistle in silver metal. (Other ranks wore an all-metal grenade.) Belt-plate – in silver on a frosted gilt rectangular plate, a wreath of thistles; within the wreath, the figure of St Andrew with cross; on the wreath at the bottom, a silver scroll inscribed 'Royal Scots Fusiliers'.

The regulations stated that Scottish regiments wearing trews were to be dressed as infantry, with the exception of the doublet and trews and other Scottish items. However, none of the three regiments adopted the white cross-belt but suspended the claymore from a waist-belt. There was

PLATE 46 *Officers of the Royal Scots, 1904, in the Kilmarnock bonnet which replaced the spiked blue cloth infantry helmet.*

no change in the dress in the 1894 regulations except that the alteration in title of the King's Own Borderers was noted. In 1887, as a result of the Scottish Borderers Militia being made the 3rd Battalion, the title was changed to the King's Own Scottish Borderers. Plate 45 shows a group of NCOs and men of the Royal Scots Fusiliers in 1896 in various types of dress including full dress, serge frock and the dress of the drum-major and piper. Before the end of the century, there had been various alterations in the tartan. In 1897, the King's Own Scottish Borderers gave up the government tartan and adopted the Leslie tartan, while before that date the Royal Scots Fusiliers, who had never been entirely happy about adopting tartan, added a blue line to the government set.

Dress Regulations for 1900, issued during the South African War, described khaki foreign-service dress, which was also adopted by the non-kilted Lowland regiments (see p 95). The regulations noted that the Royal Scots and the King's Own Scottish Borderers were not to wear the forage cap but instead to wear the glengarry 'of a pattern similar to that worn by the men', which was blue with a red, white and blue diced band and a

black silk rosette on the left side, to which the badge was fitted. The regulations also note that the Royal Scots Fusiliers were now wearing a shoulder-belt 3in wide with slings to carry the claymore in the Highland regimental fashion. The other two regiments followed this lead in 1903 and in the regulations of the following year were noted as wearing shoulder-belts 'as for kilted regiments'.

The Royal Scots altered their tartan in 1901 from the government to that of Hunting Stewart and in 1903 both the Royal Scots and the King's Own Scottish Borderers were given permission to stop wearing the infantry blue cloth helmet and in its place wore a Kilmarnock bonnet with plume. This is shown in plate 46, with officers in full dress.

The 1904 *Dress Regulations* ordered a frock coat for wear in undress by the officers of the three Lowland regiments. This was in blue cloth with a stand collar and a double row of seven regimental-pattern buttons. There were two buttons at the waist behind, one at the waist each side of the skirts and one on a panel in the middle of the skirts.

In 1913, in common with the rest of the infantry, shoulder-straps on the men's doublets were altered to the facing colour and, in the following year, full dress was returned to store on mobilisation, never to be used again by the bulk of the army.

Scottish Rifles 1881–1914

The 1881 army reforms created a Scottish rifle regiment from the combination of the 26th (Cameronians) and the 90th (Perthshire Volunteers) Light Infantry. The problem of uniform needed obvious thought. It should be green as the regiment was a rifle one, yet, because it was Scottish, it had to reflect its origins. The answer was a unique uniform combining the various points mentioned above. The doublet was chosen complete with Inverness skirts and gauntlet cuffs but in green cloth with the facings in green, the same colour as the doublet. Trews were worn and these were of government tartan. Plate 47 shows a colour sergeant of the regiment c 1885. The helmet, with leather-bound rounded peak for other ranks, was covered in green cloth and had silver metal fittings consisting of spike and cross-piece, rosettes each side, chin-chain and regimental badge worn on the front. As with other rifle regiments wearing the helmet, the plate was a complete departure from the normal star pattern with crown above in brass worn by the infantry rank and file and the two Scottish Lowland regiments. The plate, worn by the officers also on their helmet – which differed in that it had a metal-bound pointed peak and a strip down the centre at the back – was

> A thistle wreath surmounted by a crown. On the leaves of the wreath, the battles of the regiment. Within the wreath, a mullet, a bugle with strings. On a tablet to the right of the wreath, the Dragon of China; on a tablet to the left, the Sphinx. On the bottom of the wreath a scroll inscribed 'The Scottish Rifles'.

The other ranks wore black leather equipment of the normal infantry pattern in use with black leather straps to the waterbottle and black canvas haversack. The belt had a white metal snake-type fastening in place of the usual 'universal' locket bearing the royal crest and motto.

Officers wore the doublet as well but it was laced across the front in similar fashion to the tunic worn by officers of rifle regiments but in flat braid without loops or olivets. The skirts and cuffs were Highland pattern with three button-loops of black Russia braid and black netted buttons. Shoulder-straps were of 'black chain gimp' with badges of rank in bronze. The method of denoting rank by the addition of extra braid on the collar, cuffs and skirts was as in the Highland regiments.

PLATE 47 *Colour sergeant, Cameronians, Scottish Rifles (26th and 90th), in green doublet, green cloth helmet (replaced in 1892 by a shako) and Black Watch tartan trews which were replaced in 1892 by Douglas tartan.*

The only buttons bearing the regimental badge – a crowned bugle horn within a thistle wreath – were worn, in bronze, on the greatcoat. The sword-belt, worn over the doublet, was in black patent leather with a frosted silver plate, with a thistle wreath around a crowned mullet and a bugle horn on the base of the wreath. As this was a rifle regiment, officers wore a black patent-leather cross-belt and pouch, the former ornamented with a regimental badge and whistle and chain in silver and the latter with a thistle on the flap, again in silver. Mounted officers wore breeches and boots and a black patent-leather sabretache with thistle on the flap.

The distinction of the diced band on the forage cap accorded to the 26th (see Chapter 3, p 79) was not continued in the Scottish Rifles and they wore a Rifle-green cloth cap with $1\frac{1}{2}$in band of black thistle lace with a braided figure and netted button on the crown, a black leather chin-strap but no peak. Other ranks wore a dark-green side cap as worn in other rifle regiments.

In 1891, the regiment gave up the government tartan for trews in the Douglas tartan. In 1893, both officers and other ranks gave up wearing the helmet. It was the only one of the three rifle regiments still wearing it, the Rifle Brigade and the King's Royal Rifle Corps having adopted the busby, and a green cloth shako, similar in shape to that worn by the Highland Light Infantry. The officers' doublet was also altered and the cumbersome bars of lace disappeared from the front and it was fastened with eight regimental-pattern buttons. The doublet now assumed the exact appearance of that worn by Highland officers, except of course it was in Rifle-green cloth. Shoulder-cords were abolished and Rifle-green cloth shoulder-straps substituted. The black mohair braid was now described as black thistle pattern and adorned the collar of the doublet and was used on the cuff and skirts to denote rank. The description of the new doublet appeared in *Dress Regulations* 1894, which also described the shako or chaco. It was similar in shape to that worn by the Highland Light Infantry and was in Rifle-green with a band of black braid at the top and bottom. It also had the corded lines over the peak in black braid. On the front was a bronze stringed bugle horn and above, on a corded boss, a bronze mullet. A $6\frac{1}{2}$in plume of black egret feathers, with black vulture-feather base, was worn in the top front. Rank and file wore a similar shako but of lower quality. The old helmet plate continued to be worn on the white foreign-service helmet.

The cap lines fastened to the back of the cap and went around the neck, hooking up on the left breast. Other ranks, although having the cords over the peak as in the Highland Light Infantry, did not have cap lines which went over the body. The other ranks' shako was similar in design but without the black braid binding.

The officer's patrol jacket, which was adopted when the regiment became a rifle one in 1881, was in green cloth (serge for hot weather) with 1in-wide mohair braid around the body and skirts, and traced inside with black Russia braid forming 'three eyes at the top, and 2 eyes at the bottom'. On each side of the front there were five loops of black cord, fastened with olivets. The jacket was similar to that worn in the infantry and other Highland regiments except for the colour (see plate 28).

The shell jacket, which later became the mess jacket, was also in green cloth with 1in-wide mohair braid around the body, 'forming barrels or dummies at the bottom of the back seams', which were trimmed with black gimp chain with a crow's-foot knot at the top and an Austrian knot at the bottom, with a tracing of Russia braid each side. On the later mess jacket, mentioned in the 1894 regulations, there were five loops of black square cord on each side of the breast with netted caps and drops, fastening with olivets.

In foreign-service dress, the regiment wore khaki but with the trews – until after 1900, when khaki trousers were issued in their place.

In 1900, a new edition of *Dress Regulations* reverted to the old pattern of shell jacket for the mess jacket with the plain front and the five olivets on the left side of the front. The 1904 regulations, while describing the new service dress, altered nothing in the officer's full-dress uniform but specified that the only garment for undress was the patrol jacket previously worn.

The other ranks continued to wear the same pattern of doublet, with embroidered 'S.R.' on the shoulder-straps until the abolition of full dress for rank and file.

Pipers of the Scottish Rifles had worn flat bonnets and government tartan trews until 1887, when they became dressed like Highland pipers, wearing glengarries and the kilt in Douglas tartan. The doublet was green and, in common with other regimental pipers, they wore a black baldrick with engraved silver buckle and black waist-belt with silver buckle. The tartan worn by the pipers was always the Douglas, even when the 26th, prior to 1881, had their 'unofficial' pipers (see Chapter 3, p 82).

The Cameronians abandoned their full dress for khaki for ever in 1914, but even so, during the first few months of the war, field officers were still wearing Douglas-tartan breeches and glengarries.

Chapter 5 Service Dress
1902–1918

The service dress introduced by two army orders in 1902 (one for officers, one for other ranks) was intended for all arms of the service. The jacket was common to both cavalry and infantry – Highland and Scottish infantry and rifles excepted, for they wore a slightly different design. It was to be the same colour as issued to rank and file, with a turn-down Prussian collar fastened with hooks and eyes. It was single-breasted and had an expanding pleat in the centre of the back. There were two breast pockets with a central expanding pleat, flaps and bronze buttons and two expanding pockets below the waist with pleats at the side. There were five bronze regimental-pattern buttons down the front. The shoulder-straps, which were removable, were in the same coloured cloth with a variety of coloured braid trimming to distinguish infantry from cavalry and rifles from fusiliers. The original system of ranking introduced in Army Order 40 of 1902 was not only unsightly but complicated, involving as it did various lines of braid and knots, making the sleeve of a lt-colonel a forest of lines and knots covering almost half of the sleeve. The ranking system was as follows: second-lieutenant – cuffs edged all round in drab braid with a crow's-foot knot at the point; lieutenant – the same but with a double line of braid ending in knots each side of the point; captain – as for lieutenant but with the central knot at the point surmounted by a double line of braid and knot; major – as for captain but with two additional

double lines of braid between the outer line and the centre line and reaching higher; lt-colonel – as for major but with the central double line of braid surmounted by another double line terminating in a knot.

Army Order 261 of November 1902 abolished this system and introduced cuff ranking. This consisted, for cavalry and for infantry, Highland and Scottish regiments excepted, of a round cuff ringed in chevron lace with a slashed flap edged in the same lace and decorated by the usual badges of rank, stars and crowns. The higher the rank, the extra number of bands of lace that went round the cuff. In the cavalry, Bedford-cord breeches and leather boots and leggings were worn.

In the Scottish regiments, the service-dress jacket was similar to that described above but with gauntlet-shaped cuff and cut away in front to clear the sporran. When, in November 1902, the improved system of ranking was introduced, it was worn on the gauntlet cuff on the outward-facing side, the top edge augmented by extra bands of lace for higher ranks. The head-dress for Scottish regiments was the glengarry while other officers of infantry and those of the cavalry wore a forage cap with peak in the same coloured cloth as the jacket. It had a brown leather chin-strap and regimental badge on the front.

In 1904, a new edition of *Dress Regulations* was published, which described the khaki service dress and the

PLATE 48 *NCOs and men, 1st Battalion, Seaforth Highlanders (72nd and 78th), France, 1915. Note the khaki Balmoral bonnet and the fact that only the regimental sergeant-major on the left is wearing the Scottish-pattern service-dress jacket. Note also the khaki kilt covers.*

improved ranking system. At the same time, the removable shoulder-straps were dispensed with and plaited worsted braid shoulder-cords adopted. Officers were distinguished by wearing bronze collar badges on the service dress.

In 1913, Army Order 279 introduced a jacket with open collar, lapels with collar badges and shirt and tie in place of the previous pattern. In 1915, officers were given the choice of wearing their badges of rank either on the cuff or on the shoulder-strap in bronze. When worn on the shoulder, cuffs were ordered to be pointed. In 1920, Army Order 539 abolished cuff ranking and ordered that badges of rank in bronze would be worn on the shoulder-straps in service dress.

Other ranks' service dress consisted, in Highland regiments and Lowland units, of a jacket, the glengarry and kilt with khaki hose and gaiters or trews and puttees. The jacket was described as in drab-mixture serge with a turned-down rolled collar, two breast pockets with pleats and two side pockets with flaps. On each shoulder were sewn reinforcing 'rifle patches' and there were removable shoulder-straps. Regiments were distinguished by having the title embroidered in white on red cloth curved strip and sewn on the upper arm. A separate embroidered numeral was sewn beneath to distinguish the battalion. In Scottish line and rifle regiments, the front was rounded to clear the sporran. In the cavalry, the same pattern was worn. The Scots Greys other ranks wore the side cap until 1905, when a khaki peaked cap, similar to that worn by officers since 1902, was introduced. In place of the glengarry, Balmoral bonnets were issued in 1914 and in the following year ones in drab were replacing the blue bonnets. As they were greatly disliked they were frequently being 'lost' by the men. The bonnet was made of serge cloth pieced together instead of the knitted material (thrum).

In March 1916, steel helmets were introduced for active service and manoeuvres.

Shoulder-straps were soon replaced with shoulder-cords which in turn gave way in 1907 to shoulder-straps with the regimental title in metal on the straps, instead of on cloth patches.

During World War I, this was the pattern of jacket worn but, on occasions, the normal infantry-pattern jacket was issued to Scottish infantry regiments in place of the cut-away pattern (plate 48).

With the new service dress, the Slade-Wallace was worn but in 1903 a new pattern of equipment was introduced for the army (plate 49). This pattern, an entirely new idea, was made in brown leather. During the South African War the Mills Woven Cartridge Belt Company of London under the direction of Mr William Lindsey had supplied the War Office with belts and bandoliers, web straps for rifles and waterbottles, all of which had done excellently under active-service conditions and the company entertained hopes that they would soon be able to introduce all-web equipment for the army. It was found, however, that there was a great need to increase the number of rounds carried by the infantryman and a light flimsy throw-away bandolier was made by the company to answer this need. Most of the bandoliers were, however, used as a permanent item of equipment, resulting in the bandoliers falling apart with use and the loss of thousands of rounds of ammunition. When the subject of new equipment to take clips of cartridges for the new shortened Lee-Enfield rifle came up after the war, webbing was excluded from consideration, having been condemned by many of the generals, including Lord Kitchener.

The 1903 equipment, shown in wear in India in 1906 in plate 49, consisted of a leather bandolier with five pockets, worn over the left shoulder and a waist-belt (in the plate the old white Slade-Wallace belt and bayonet frog are being worn) in brown leather with two similar pouches each side. The valise was abolished and the greatcoat carried folded high on the back and the mess tin on the

PLATE 49 *Privates, Highland Light Infantry (71st and 74th), in drill-order shirt sleeves, India, 1906. Notice the regimental flash in tartan on the left side of the helmet.*

back of the belt. The haversack and waterbottle were carried on separate straps across the body.

However, after repeated attempts, the Mills company managed at last to interest the Royal Navy in a trial and in 1905 received a visit from Major A. R. Burrows of the Royal Irish Fusiliers, who put forward a new design of equipment. The major's ideas and those of the company were amalgamated, resulting in an extensive trial being made by regiments at home and in India. The 'Mills-Burrows' equipment proved to be so superior over any other previous pattern that in December 1907 it was approved by the Army Council and on 30 January 1908 was approved by King Edward VII. The new equipment consisted of a 3in wide waist-belt, with brass buckle and a set of pouches fitted each side of the buckle, consisting of five pouches arranged two above three. To the belt, behind the pouches, were fitted two braces that passed over the shoulder and crossed at the back, fastening to two buckles sewn to the back of the belt. On the left side of the belt was fitted a bayonet frog, with fitting to take the helve of the entrenching tool and to the 'loose' ends of the cross-belt on the same side was fitted the haversack. On the opposite side on the same 'loose' straps were fitted the waterbottle and the entrenching-tool holder. On the braces at the back, attached to brass sliders, was strapped the large pack. The great advantage of the equipment, apart from its scientific design and material, was that it could be put on or taken off in one piece.

The War Office placed their first order for 15,000 sets in March 1908 and thereafter the army was slowly issued with the new equipment.

On the outbreak of war, the BEF was equipped entirely with the 'pattern 1908' equipment but during the early stages of the war, when new armies were being raised, it was found that there was not enough of this equipment available. As a stop gap, the old bandolier equipment was reissued, mainly to Territorial battalions and about a million sets of all-leather '1908' equipment

PLATE 50 *Trooper, Royal Scots Greys, in full marching order, 1918. Note the wealth of equipment carried including hay, pickets, sword bayonet, rifle and extra 'horse bandolier' with spare ammunition.*

made, the only difference being that there was one large pouch each side on the belt – similar to the old Slade-Wallace pattern – and that web haversack and pack were used. Some of this equipment found its way out to France with some regiments, although it was intended mainly for training.

In the cavalry, the bandolier of the 1903 equipment was worn with service dress and continued to be worn throughout World War I, an extra bandolier being issued for putting round the horse's neck. Plate 50 shows a trooper of the Scots Greys in full marching order in 1918, complete with the helmet that replaced all other forms of head-dress in 1916, sword, rifle signal flags and so on.

Appendix

WEAPONS

This short appendix is intended to give the reader some basic information on weapons carried by the regiments in this book which were purely of a Scottish nature and not carried by other regiments of the British Army. In the 2nd Dragoons, the weapons carried by the officers and men were standard with those carried by other dragoon regiments.

The various independent companies – and later the 43rd – were equipped by the government with muskets, bayonets and broadswords and it appears that a special pattern of musket was issued. In 1757, the Board of Ordnance decided to keep a stock of weapons in the Tower of London for emergencies, amongst which were to be 'Carbines with Bayonets for Artillery and Highlanders'. By 1775, this carbine seems to have been replaced by the standard flintlock infantry musket and, from then on, Scottish regiments carried the same long arm as other line regiments.

Swords had been abandoned by infantry privates in 1768 but were retained by Highlanders and grenadiers. In 1776 Highlanders abandoned their swords, only sergeants retaining them. Highland officers carried broadswords from an early period but they were not mentioned in *Dress Regulations* until 1831, the previous edition of 1822 ordering the standard infantry sword. The basket-hilt was later reserved for full-dress wear and a cross-hilt of regimental pattern introduced for other occasions. Field officers latter adopted a half basket-hilt and this can be seen in plate 42. Lowland regiments adopted the claymore in 1881 while the Scottish Rifles adopted the rifle pattern sword, unofficially substituting a mullet with thistles in the cartouche in place of the crowned bugle horn.

All metal pistols had been carried by Highlanders and these were used by the Highland regiments raised in the eighteenth century but were paid for by the regiment. By 1757 the situation seems to have changed as in that year Montgomery's and Fraser's Highlanders were allowed 1,080 'side pistols', although the former had already procurred his and was allowed a monetary grant in lieu.

This grant seems to have been the usual practice but the Board of Ordnance later demanded proof of purchase. In 1762 when granting Colonel Murray Keith £1. 15. 7 per pair they added that pistols of the Scottish type had been made in Birmingham at 18s per pair. The Board decided to issue pistols from the Tower but in 1775, the 42nd were given a grant as there were no serviceable Scottish pistols in store.

By 1795, Highland regiments were no longer wearing the all metal pistol but they continued to be carried by officers in levee dress although they were never mentioned in *Dress Regulations*. Fig 14 shows an all metal pistol for the 92nd made in about 1848 by Henry Wilkinson, London.

FIGURE 14 *Officer's levee dress, all-metal pistol, 92nd Highlanders, c 1848 (from a drawing in the pattern book of Wilkinson & Son).*

Highland regiments were allowed to wear dirks but these were supplied at the expense of the regiment or the men. The men seem to have abandoned the dirk in about 1776 although sergeants and officers continued to carry them. Plate 14 shows a sergeant of the 42nd wearing a dirk with carved 'bog wood' grip in a leather scabbard. The top is flat and could possibly have born a regimental device or number or crown. Pipers, who were not officially sanctioned until 1854, wore dirks provided by the officers but after 1881, when Lowland regiments were permitted to have pipers, not charged to the public, the Ordnance issued a pipers' dirk which had a carved grip (later changed to dermatine because of expense) with a plain blade, flat top bearing a raised crown and scabbard with four mounts but no knife or fork.

Officers' dirks were more ornate and were of regimental pattern (fig 15). Although *Dress Regulations* mentioned that they should be gilt mounted, some regiments preferred silver. In 1881, the numbers which were used on the blade and on the top mounts gave way to badges. Lowland regiments did not adopt the dirk, the only non-kilted regiment to wear it being the Highland Light Infantry.

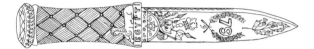

FIGURE 16   *Skean dhu, 79th Highlanders, c 1848 (from a drawing in the pattern book of Wilkinson & Son).*

The *Skean dhu*, from the Gallic meaning black knife, was of a regimental pattern with the mounts matching those of the dirk. Those worn by pipers were plain with white metal mounts while the officer's version were usually elaborate and carried a regimental badge or honour on the grip (fig 16).

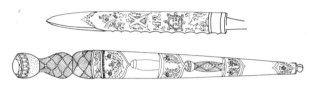

FIGURE 15. *42nd Highlanders dirk, c 1860 (from a drawing in the pattern book of Wilkinson & Son).*

FIGURE 17   Buttons: (first row, left to right) *2nd Dragoons, c 1800; Royal North British Dragoons, 1835–77; 1st Foot, 1860; Royal Scots Fusiliers (21st), 1881; King's Own Scottish Borderers (25th), 1887; Scottish Rifles (26th and 90th), 1881.* (Second row) *42nd Foot, 1810–81; 73rd Foot, 1816–81; 71st Foot, 1820–81; 74th Foot, 1820–81; 72nd Foot, 1800–81; 78th Foot, 1825–81.* (Third row) *75th Foot, 1810–81; 92nd Foot, 1800–81; Gordon Highlanders (75th and 92nd), 1881; 79th Foot, 1855–81; 91st Foot, 1830–63; 93rd Foot, 1820–81.*

Bibliography

MANUSCRIPT SOURCES: UNIFORMS

LAWSON, C. C. P. 'Manuscript Notes on British Uniforms', National Army Museum, London
REYNOLDS, P. W. 'Military Costume of the Eighteenth and Nineteenth Centuries', Victoria and Albert Museum, London
WILKINSON, Henry (later Wilkinson Sword Ltd.). 'Military Uniform Pattern Books 1840–1910', Wilkinson-Latham Collection
HOLLIES-SMITH, Captain R. G. Collection, 'Notes on Military Uniforms'

PUBLISHED SOURCES: UNIFORMS

ADAMS, Frank. *The Clans, Septs and Regiments of the Scottish Highlands* (Edinburgh, 7th ed 1965)
ALMACK, Edward. *The History of the Second Dragoons, Royal Scots Greys* (c 1908)
BROWNE, Arthur Neil Edmonstone. *Notes on the Dress of the Seventy-First Regiment* (1935)
CANNON, Richard. *Historical Records of the British Army: 2nd Dragoons* (1837); *1st Foot* (1847); *21st Foot* (1849); *42nd Foot* (1845); *71st Foot* (1852); *72nd Foot* (1848); *73rd Foot* (1851); *74th Foot* (1850); *92nd Foot* (1851)
CARMAN, W. Y. *British Military Uniforms* (1957)
——. *Head Dresses of the British Army – Cavalry* (Sutton, 1968)
CARTER, Thomas (ed). *Historical Record of the Twenty-Six, Cameronian Regiment* (1867)
CHICHESTER and BURGES-SHORT. *Records and Badges of the British Army* (Aldershot, 1900)
GROVES, Lt-Colonel Percy. *History of the First Battalion Princess Louise's Argyll and Sutherland Highlanders (91st Foot)* (1894)
——. *Illustrated Histories of the Scottish Regiments: 2nd Dragoons (Royal Scots Greys)* (1893); *Black Watch (Royal Highlanders)* (1893)
HASWELL MILLER, A. E. and DAWNEY, N. P. *Military Drawings and Paintings in the Royal Collection*, 2 vols (1966, 1970)
HOLDING, T. H. *Uniforms of the British Army, Navy and Court* (1894)
JAMESON, Captain Robert. *Historical Record of the Seventy-Ninth Foot or Cameron Highlanders* (Edinburgh, 1863)
KELTIE, J. S. (ed). *History of the Scottish Highlands, Highland Clans and Highland Regiments* (1887)
LAWSON, C. C. P. *A History of the Uniforms of the British Army*, 5 vols (1940–67)
LETHERN, A. A. *The Development of the Mills Woven Cartridge Belt 1877–1956* (1956)
LUARD, Lt-Colonel John. *A History of the Dress of the British Soldier* (1852)
MOLLO, John. *Waterloo Uniforms 1: Cavalry* (1973)
MONEY-BARNES, Major and KENNEDY, C. *The Uniforms and History of the Scottish Regiments* (1960)
NEVILLE, R. *British Military Prints* (1909)
PARKYN, Major H. G. *Shoulder Belt Plates and Buttons* (Aldershot, 1956)
SCOBIE, Major I. H. McK. *The Scottish Regiments of the British Army* (Edinburgh 1942)
STEWART, Colonel D. *Sketches of the Character and Present State of the Highlands of Scotland* (Edinburgh 1822)

SYM, Colonel J. *The Seaforth Highlanders 1788–1954* (1962)
THORBURN, W. A. *Uniforms of the Scottish Infantry 1740–1900* (Edinburgh, 1970)
WILKINSON-LATHAM, Robert and Christopher. *Cavalry Uniforms of Britain and the Commonwealth* (1969)
——. *Infantry Uniforms of Britain and the Commonwealth*, 2 vols (1969, 1970)

PUBLISHED SOURCES: WEAPONS

BLACKMORE, Howard L. *British Military Firearms* (1961)
WILKINSON-LATHAM, J. *British Cut and Thrust Weapons* (Newton Abbot, 1971)

OFFICIAL PUBLICATIONS

Dress Regulations for the Army for 1822, 1831, 1834, 1846, 1855, 1857, 1861, 1864, 1874, 1883, 1894, 1900, 1904, 1911, 1934
A Collection of Regulations, Orders and Instructions (1788)
Standing Orders and Regulations for the Army in Ireland (1794; repr 1969)

JOURNALS

Bulletin of the Military Historical Society
Journal of the Society for Army Historical Research
Navy and Army Illustrated
Red Hackle
Soldier Magazine
Tradition

During the research for this book, a large number of regimental histories were consulted but most contained little on the subject of uniforms.

INDEX